FROM
CIRCUS
—TO—
PURPOSE

by

Brian D. Williams

From Circus to Purpose

Blue Café Books for
www.carladupont.com
Atlanta, GA
Printed in the USA.

ISBN: 979-8-218-62476-7

Credits
Editorial: Carla DuPont
Cover Design: Garrett Myers

Acknowledgements

This book would not be possible without the incredible circle of loved ones, friends, and supporters I have around me. God placed the idea of this book on my heart during one of my deepest isolations. I thank God for sharing so many principles with me and allowing me to rediscover so many things in His word. Through the years, I've had a passion for writing, thankful that I'm now able to have purpose in something I love.

God, I acknowledge you, trust you, and love you with every fiber of my being.

Thank you to my wife, Charnell, for never being impressed with anything, LOL. It motivated me to only do things that made me happy to complete, and I needed to figure that out. Although we've never discussed it, I feel like you knew that. You've always been supportive of my MANY, MANY, MANY endeavors. I appreciate the partnership and teamwork approach we take against the world. I am beyond thankful to God for trusting me with you. Without you, this is not possible.

To my mother, thank you for loving me unconditionally.

My whole life I always had you which means the world to me. I hope I make you proud.

To my father, you are a GOAT in my eyes. At times I feel like a carbon copy of you professionally. I appreciate the blueprint you left to this generation of Williamses. You recognized things in me as a kid that it took me years to figure out.

Thank you to my older sibling, Tracy, for the wise counsel and allowing me to vent enough professionally to even write this book.

To my other older sibling, Bobby, you have always had my back, and I appreciate that. You are a great big brother to me.

To Ajah, I see a lot of myself in you. I would like to believe you are the fun parts of me, and I enjoy having you in my life. You are so talented with your hands; I can't wait to see what you choose to develop.

Londyn, you are the creator. I'm happy that you are realizing your limitless potential.

Brilynn aka Rocky aka B...thank you for your HUGE heart. You are special in so many ways and your brilliance truly keeps our family intact.

Last but not least, Bryson. You are the light, the pinnacle

of what I always wanted to become. A perfect storm of humor, charm, intelligence, and your dad's good looks. Keep going, son. You all were heavily on my mind throughout the process of writing this book. You all have motivated me to discover my gift so I can help you each discover yours.

Well, kids... I have the blueprint! I can't wait to share more as you all develop into your greatness.

To Gloria Williams, Alex Padgett, Cedric Ward, Jonathan Glasco, and Pastor Tommy, thank you for the support to continue the mission.

And finally, thanks to the men who constantly attend our men's group "Man of Means" and provide feedback on the concepts of this book. This book is truly a group effort.

Thank you to everyone who works at AccuClean, Inc. It's an honor to be your president. Each of you has taught me many life lessons in your own way.

Thank you to Dr. Grady and the members of the Word of Faith Bondage Breaker Group. It was inspiring to read the book and discuss topics with you all weekly. It provided a spiritual foundation for me to keep the Lord first while writing this book.

Last but not least, thank you, God, for never giving up on

me and remaining with me through my circus. There was once a moment where I felt I missed my opportunity to be great, but I was sadly mistaken. Therefore, I honor you for your everlasting grace.

Letter to Readers

Dear Purpose Readers,

I want to first start by saying, I've been there. Life throws enough distractions at you to keep you occupied if you aren't intentional about taking the time to figure out your purpose. That's by design. I also want to encourage you about taking a very important step towards traveling out of the fog of social media, politics, inflation, and cancel culture.

YOU MADE THE DECISION TO ACT!

Taking a step followed by another helps you arrive at the answers. Have you noticed that any time you move towards something without a clear picture of what to expect once you arrive, you travel with hesitance? Delaying your moment to determine if this is the place you are supposed to be further delays your purpose confirmation. Before you answer your mission, you have to first know there's a mission. After reading or listening to this book, you will have clear instructions on how to find your purpose in life.

I would like to congratulate you on not ignoring the red flags in your vision and traveling a road of self-discovery to change your trajectory. This is a solo journey that no one can take for you but you. Thank you for choosing yourself and creating a better you. Have the confidence and determination to start and finish. You deserve to be able to operate at unimaginable levels. You are one of a kind, like no other. There has never been and will never be anyone like you. Reveal your unique talents and gifts to the world while honoring God. This is one of the most important tasks in life which is why I'm often surprised it's never been a part of a high school curriculum. Here I am to explain that age, race, or gender play no factor in the distribution of purpose inside of us. Continue your journey regardless of when you decided to start.

While going through a season of drought and isolation, I discovered a plan that transformed my life. If I can do this, literally anyone can. I've experienced great successes and accomplished many goals and started over after failing more times than I can count. I'm now able to focus on doing the things I love while being compensated very well for it. Also, I wake up in a peaceful state of mind, free from anxiety.

I've decided to share my progress in *From Circus to Purpose* with you while outlining how I discovered the most important thing about myself...why am I here?

Contents

Introduction

Let's start here...what's a circus? A traveling company of acrobats, clowns, and other entertainers that give performances, typically in a large tent, in a series of different places. While I was never a part of the staff of the Ringling Bros., some nights I was definitely a clown. Disguised as being happy, I was acrobatic with deceit. I could twist the truth with the best of them. And I was also an entertainer; the larger the crowd, the better. A people pleaser who did things to get others to validate my self-esteem when it was at its lowest. My self-esteem and confidence were unable to operate independently. I needed others to refuel it occasionally.

Unknowingly, I created the Brian Williams Circus. Believing an abundance of money would make me happy, I was in bondage. Similar to the tiger-taming ringmaster, I did dangerous things for the applause of people who never cared about me. Walking a tightrope so thin that one mistake, could land me in prison or lead me to death before age 40. I was amid chaos having no idea what my purpose was. I had nothing to work towards. Because I lacked direction, I had no way to define my version of success. I spent most of my 20s running a family-owned business, creating a few business ventures, and failing at maintaining meaningful relationships.

I was in the church often enough to know what God was doing but was unable to figure out what He wanted for me. I told myself that I needed to spend more time building a relationship with Him. However, because I couldn't recognize His voice, hearing from Him felt like it should be mythical. I would try and quit.

Inside the circus, it's loud with your favorite song on repeat. The spotlight is on you and it's your job to entertain others at the expense of your sense of self. In order to entertain others, you may morph into something unrecognizable. Willing to do anything to get that high five, a like on Instagram, or a follow on Twitter. And while I would change to make myself more palatable to others, internally I was becoming miserable. The circus can be fun until the show is over and everyone else exits the stands leaving you by yourself. An overwhelming feeling of loneliness would come over me some nights. Clinging to people similar to me who couldn't help me because they had been overpowered in their battle.

To avoid this feeling, I needed others to constantly validate me, even if they just told me the previous week I was smart, handsome, a leader, ambitious, and a good critical thinker. My memory was so short with the recollection of compliments. There was a show every day with me; grab your tickets! In the midst of trying not to feel loneliness or depression, I hurt people close to me. Intermittently the circus show damages and hurts people. Regardless of whether it was your intention to harm someone, they may never return to your big tent. The same people who came to support can sometimes be hurt just by being there for you. The devil fooled me into believing because of the circus around me and the sins I committed that I was no longer in God's favor. He told me daily I had my shot to fulfill God's will, and I'd missed it. Satan told me to just live the rest of my life as best as I saw fit; you can't fix the past, it's over for you.

I wrote this book for the sinner who is lost. You can regain what was promised, and God is so brilliant that He can use what you did wrong to make your story give Him all the glory. Someone will see you operating in your purpose and know this has to be aligned by God. They will know it is now possible for them because of you.

Today, I stand before you close to God, happily married, a proud father of four, and the best entrepreneur in Atlanta. So I humbly present to you myself similar to Jesus presenting Himself after leaving the tomb. Scarred but not ashamed. Showing that through the grace of God, I have overcome. Do not conform but be transformed by the renewing of your mind. *From Circus to Purpose* means you can go from a life of chaos, confusion, depression, and loneliness to a life of meaning, purpose, fulfillment, and happiness. Dedicating time to figure out your purpose allows your time to be better utilized in the kingdom and free from materialistic bondage.

I promise if you read this book in its entirety and apply the principles within, you will transform your life. I urge you to continue this book with vigor until you have completely applied everything within. Once you have identified what brings you joy, discovering your purpose is the next step. It's important to remember that your purpose isn't necessarily something heroic or grandiose; it can simply be doing something meaningful and worthwhile in whatever context feels right for you. Your purpose is unique to you and may even change over time as you grow and learn more about yourself. Remaining open-minded and focusing on what motivates you will get you through this book.

Remember, discovering your purpose doesn't have to be a linear process. It may take some trial and error before you feel like you've found your "calling." You have the resources and the power within to make meaningful connections with others, become more self-aware, and ultimately discover your life's true purpose. The process involves patience, courage, and resilience — all of which will help you uncover the seed gift inside of YOU. Therefore, don't be afraid to explore different paths or make mistakes as you learn more about yourself. You have now crossed the threshold to purpose...enjoy the process!

FROM CIRCUS TO PURPOSE

CHAPTER 1

○ ○ ○

Taking Inventory

"I cry out to God Most High, to God who will
fulfill his purpose for me."

Psalms 57:2 NLT

Take inventory of your life.

To understand what's necessary for you to find your purpose, you must take an inventory of your life. Doing a personal inventory of your life means acknowledging your weaknesses and strengths; appreciating what you are naturally great at and determining ways you can improve on your weak areas. Making a complete list of your inner contents is the seed to the tree of purpose. We have all done inventory in some forms of life. It could be as simple as looking at how much is in the refrigerator or jotting down a list of the household items that you need to purchase before you go to the store. This is not a quick process that you can get done in a day. It will take time to concentrate and focus on every aspect of your life to date. There are four steps that you will take to begin this journey:

- Isolate
- Reflect
- Inventory
- Discover

Some may have unknowingly completed the above steps during different phases of their lives and arrived at living a life of purpose. I must stress that you have to be intentional about spending this time and investing in this four-step process.

Let me tell you a story that illustrates taking inventory of your life. One of the most impactful creators of entertainment in the 20th century was once fired from a newspaper publication. The reason he was terminated was because "he lacked creativity." After leaving, he started his own animation business called Laugh-O-Gram, but the business didn't generate enough revenue and shortly after went bankrupt. This same man traveled to Hollywood with little to no money to only face more criticism and rejection. The man was Walt Disney, one of the best film producers and entrepreneurs ever!

I want you to imagine your core values as inventory on the shelves in a grocery store. People along your journey may suggest you don't have items in your store meaning what they suggest or rumor is unimpactful while you are operating in your purpose. Yet, if you are aware of what's in your inventory, you can easily dismiss their claims of what you have – or don't have – to offer. Walt Disney continued in his purpose because he knew what was inside of him regardless of the feedback he received.

After completing this 4-step process, you will be able to navigate life with the same level of fearlessness.

Isolate

This is probably the most important step in the journey of finding your purpose. Go to a quiet place in your home that can shield you from distraction. Some people create prayer closets with lamps and floor pillows which can be a great way to isolate yourself in comfort. Other ideas can be to get a hotel for the weekend or sit in your car in a parking lot. Take the day off from work or school, trust me, this is essential. Notify your loved ones that you are taking some time to yourself. Put your phone in 'do not disturb' mode and delete social media apps off your phone.

Creating an isolated environment won't be effortless. Nor will there ever be an ideal time to schedule your isolation for clear thoughts. Instead of looking for the perfect time, intentionally make yourself available for you and unavailable for everyone else. Pray (you are going to hear me say that often) and ask God for wisdom and revelation regarding your purpose. This season of your journey may be challenging but ultimately worth the reward. It can be dark and lonely while you are in this phase, with a lot of uncertainty but I want to encourage you that this step is very important in equipping you with what's needed for this process.

I had a tutor for algebra in high school. My tutor once told me that the reason one-on-one tutoring worked so well with many is because the student and tutor were communicating directly with one another. The likelihood of you being able to understand instructions completely increases drastically. In a similar way, isolation allows you the opportunity to receive clear instructions when your attention is not divided. Isolating yourself for a long period of time can be unhealthy. Stay in the stage of isolation until you receive a certain amount of peace in your spirit. When you are at peace, there's no worry that you have no gifts or talents. There's no frustration that you are running out of time. The devil is the master of distraction, while focus is from God. There is never going to be an ideal day or time to do this. Seize the day to invest in your temporary isolation.

One of my favorite stories growing up showing the power of isolation was the Disney story, "The Lion King." Simba's dad, Mufasa, died. So, to avoid death from his Uncle Scar, Simba fled to the wilderness. Being driven out of his rightful position, Simba was in a season of isolation. There's one scene in particular that resonated with me. Simba was challenged that he didn't know who he was by the baboon named Rafiki. Looking into the water, he saw not just his physical appearance but also reflected on who he truly was and who he wanted to become.

This moment marked the beginning of his journey toward self-discovery and acceptance. It's a metaphorical representation of looking inward and facing one's own fears, doubts, and truths. Throughout the film, Mufasa served as a guiding presence for Simba, even after his death. When Simba looked into the water, he saw his father's reflection superimposed over his own. This symbolized the influence and legacy of Mufasa, reminding Simba of his father's wisdom and the values instilled in him.

After confronting his reflection and realizing the impact of his actions, Simba began to accept responsibility for his past and his role in the circle of life. This moment marked a turning point for Simba as he decided to reclaim his rightful place as the king of the Pride Lands and fulfill his destiny.

We are the righteousness of God. Sometimes it takes a season of isolation for us to remember that. There may come a time in your life when you realize you've ignored all the signs and avoided making time to discover your true purpose. Sometimes God will force your isolation because you are depending on things other than Him. I've had friends who have had unhealthy relationships with situations and possessions such as careers or cars only for that "thing" to be removed from their lives bringing them back to their true purpose.

Flip the bible open and read it randomly until something speaks to you or intrigues you to research. You can rest in complete faith because you know what God has promised you from spending time reading His word daily. With those promises, it provides a certain level of comfort that helps you gain the confidence to proceed to the next step. Speak this prayer before proceeding to the next step of reflecting.

Heavenly Father, I ask that during this time of isolation,
Where I'm spending quality time with you and your word,
That you assist and mold me for your divine intentions,

*That you allow me to identify my purpose and my
divine gift,
That you show me how to use my gift to bring more
people to you,
That you allow me to open the doors that will bring me
closer to you.
In your name I pray, Amen.*

Reflect

The second step of the process is to reflect. After praying, close your eyes and reflect on your life. Jot down your achievements, emotions, feelings, and reactions to things that have happened in your life. What have you been successful at accomplishing so far? This can be a little league championship, family complimenting about certain dishes they love for you to prepare, or how effortless it is for you to galvanize a group of people into productivity. Your gift is wrapped up in the packaging of what comes easiest to you. Most people can do many things well with the right training but let's focus on natural talent.

When you are gifted, it may be difficult for you to see it because it's normal to you. We use our gifts to fulfill the purpose of our lives. In 1 Peter 4:10, we're called to use our gifts to serve others as faithful stewards of God's grace. Meaning God doesn't give you the gift for your own benefit although many of us have abused our gifts. God crafted a purpose for you, so take note of who you are by reflecting inwardly.

For this step, I asked a few guys from a men's group I started called Men of Wisdom to write a list of things they like to do. After they jotted down a few things, I asked them to write next to each thing why they like to do it. One guy listed he liked to play basketball, and his reason was because he enjoyed practicing moves in his back-yard so when he played at the gym, he could execute them. Was his gift basketball? Maybe not, he never played at a collegiate level. But he was able to prepare plans and execute them. That gift can be used in a myriad of environments. Pay very close attention to what you like to do and what you do well while reflecting. Focus on one aspect of your life at a time. You may start by reflect-ing on your relationships, career, personal growth, or any other area important to you.

Do a little activity for me. Imagine someone was creating a biopic on your life. Write down three positive life events that instantly stand out to you as achievements, an important milestone, a graduation, or recognition for a job well done that you'd like included. Then, write down three life events that are a part of your story you wouldn't want people to see. These are the parts that if your biopic were shown in a theater, would make you cringe or you'd want to fast forward through them. You know they happened, but you've healed and would ra-ther not revisit it. Or maybe you are still fighting what happened and feel guilty about it. What you learn and ex-perience in your triumphant moments and unpleasant events in your life is invaluable. These events are a part of your personality, interests, morals, and provide insight into you as a person. God has a way of showing us His divine intentions throughout our life from a child to adulthood. Your purpose is connected, just pay attention to the details. Your gift is connected to your three major life events.

Positive Life Events (examples: graduation, weight loss, marriage, home purchase, GPA)

1. _____

_____

2. _____

_____

3. _____

_____

Fast Forward Moments (car accident, abuse, arrest, infidelity, friendship ended, family feud)

1. _____

_____

2. _____

_____

3. _____

_____

Next, review these events and moments to see if there are any similarities. Working with a few guys in my men's group, I've noticed that sometimes the fast forward moments create positive life events. Or early in their childhood, they had multiple fast forward moments that created positive life events. The reverse could be positive life events occur before a fast forward moment approaches that helps to refocus the purpose.

This exercise simply puts your life on paper so you can spend time understanding what happened in your life and why. The word reflect is defined as throwback without absorbing it. So think deeply about your life but the objective is not to absorb yourself with past mistakes. Compare and contrast your life events to find the commonality between them. Many of us are living in the life we prayed for years ago. This exercise can help us realize the positive life events God has granted us while also showing us how fast forward moments have molded us into becoming a better Christian.

In Exodus 36, the Israelites were building a holy place for God. God equipped them with the skills to build. God delivered the instructions to Moses and those that He equipped to complete the task did so with skill. Take a moment to reflect on the unique gifts and abilities God has blessed you with, enabling you to fulfill His will effortlessly. You have what it takes. Many of us just have to take the time to think about what has happened in the past to discover the gifts that God was attempting to reveal.

Inventory

Growing up into adulthood, we are given guidance from our parents on how to navigate this world. Sometimes we are given are unintentionally bad, or unuseful tips. As adults, we have to do inventory on our lives before finding our purpose. Imagine it as a warehouse or a garage that you must declutter, clean, and organize. Inventory your core values and what's important to you. Get rid of the pieces of yourself that don't make you a better person. Two ways to rid yourself of inventory that doesn't help your personal store are to:

1. Discard the inventory and practice not using it. For example, say as a youth you were shown to meet conflict with verbal assaults or physical fights. Put into daily practice walking away from the things that don't serve you. Initially, it will be difficult, but it will form a habit that will allow you to remove this from your personal store.
2. Evaluate the reason an item is still in your personal store. Some items we store for pride and ego. Why is this item a part of your store? Is it a Christian value? If not, remove it. If the item

brings traumatic emotions, go through the healing process.

Inventory Core Values

If you won the lottery today, what cause would you support with a donation? This helps you identify things you want to impact in the world. What types of things break your heart? For example, do you get extremely sad thinking of a child who can't read or a teen who just joined a gang?

Most people want to leave the world a better place. Your purpose is connected to what you are passionate about. And inventorying the core of you will assist in discovering your calling. Core values are the fundamental beliefs that guide a person's actions and decisions. They are the guiding principles that shape a person's behavior and determine how they approach life and interact with others. Core values can vary from person-to-person, but they are typically related to a person's sense of purpose, integrity, and responsibility. They help a person understand what is important to them and motivate them to live in alignment with their values.

There are a few different ways to identify your core values:

Reflect on your experiences: Think about the times when you felt most alive, fulfilled, and authentic. What values were you upholding in those moments?

Consider your relationships: How do you want to be treated by others? What values do you hold dear in your relationships with friends, family, and loved ones?

Define your priorities: What is most important in your life? What do you want to stand for? What do you want to achieve?

Look to your role models: Who do you admire and why? What values do they embody that you would like to emulate in your own life?

Once you have identified your core values, it can be helpful to write them down and keep them in a place where you can refer back to them. This can help you stay true to your values and make decisions that are in line with them.

Some examples of core values are integrity, courage, creativity, loyalty, and compassion. While reading my bible, I learned that friendship and community were important core values to Jesus. These things were valuable to Him. He had a deep friendship with Martha, Mary, and their brother, Lazarus. He also intentionally surrounded himself with His disciples. Were these things connected to His purpose? Absolutely.

Knowing your core values and genuinely caring about

what you choose to do with your life enables you to tap into a work stamina that career workers can never reach. Today, it's possible to find people with good work ethic. But operating in your purpose with your gifts allows you to have good work stamina. Meaning good work ethic can work towards a goal but can be inconsistent. Good work stamina consistently works towards the goal without relief because of the passionate connection. It all flows together, in a sense.

Bestselling author Stephen King's first book *Carrie* was rejected by publishers 30 times. Stephen King was able to continue in his purpose because of his insatiable calling to write.

Once you have established what's important to you and what you are made of, you now know what gift you can give this world to make it a better place. If I'm a store owner, I have to determine what I have to sell first. The great thing about this is you have something that no one on Earth can sell like you…YOURSELF!

Discovery

The last step in this chapter is discovery. After you've isolated yourself to hear and to be led, reflected on your past celebrations and tribulations, taken an inventory of what's important to you and what you have in store, you must now conclude with discovery. You don't decide the will of God, you discover it. The seed of curiosity is in you, so the last step is searching for that treasure. Most are usually shocked at what they discover. Your gift has allowed you to do something so easily that you may not have realized others struggle with. I was never taught to take time to get to know myself.

If you don't know yourself, you can't grow yourself.

Most people go through life without focusing on ways to improve who they are. Instead of looking at your failures as something that can't be fixed, view them as opportunities to better yourself. View the first 18 years of your life as something that needs to be audited for accuracy. Go into discovery mode to find the things that can be improved. Isolating yourself, then reflecting on your life, taking inventory, and then going into discovery can be a painful process if you let it.

I noticed when I don't completely understand something, I'm hesitant to pursue it and procrastinate researching it. What if my purpose is something I've never tried because of fear? There's nothing God can't equip me for. I'm not waiting on Him, He's waiting on me...to develop in periods of isolation so I can hear Him clearly. Step out on faith, and His word guarantees you'll make it to the other side. My definition of discovery is all about being open to the patterns you see after reflecting in isolation. If you keep seeing 2+2 it equals 4, believe it.

Your purpose is buried deep inside of you and will only

flourish in the right environment. Most think you have to find your purpose. The truth is, you have to discover it and find the best habitat for it to grow in. It's already inside of you. Discover your special gift, and go into a place your seed can grow.

We have to agree there are certain life tasks others can't do for us. A family member can't go to school for you, no one else can get you into physical shape, and no one can find your purpose. Take some time to work on developing you. I promise you won't regret it. It's an investment that you will thank yourself for throughout your lifetime.

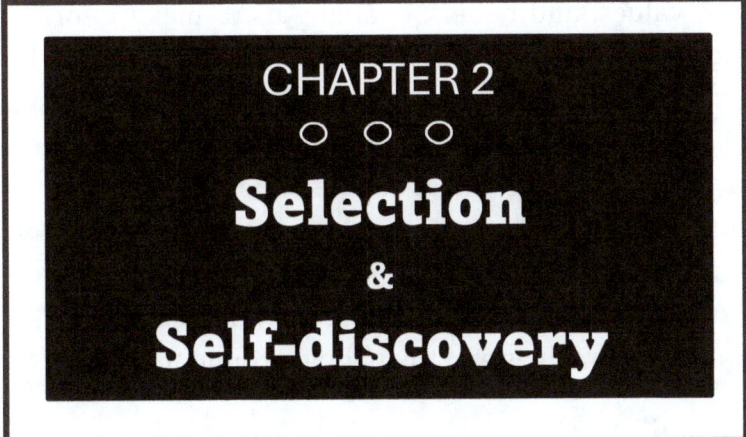

CHAPTER 2
o o o
Selection
&
Self-discovery

"Whether therefore ye eat, or drink, or
whatsoever ye do, do all to the glory of God."

1 Corinthians 10:31

F irst, let's define self-discovery. Self-discovery is an important part of personal growth, as it helps us identify our strengths and weaknesses and understand who we are. It also allows us to explore our interests, values, and beliefs, enabling us to make informed decisions about our lives. It can be a difficult process, but it can also be incredibly rewarding. The purpose of self-discovery is to gain insight into oneself, which can lead to greater self-awareness and personal growth. Through this process, we can learn more about ourselves and our purpose in life. We can also become more mindful of our thoughts and feelings, allowing us to make better decisions for ourselves and the people around us.

Self-discovery is an essential part of personal development; it can help us uncover our hidden potential. By taking the time to explore ourselves, we can gain a greater understanding of who we are and what we want out of life. With this newfound knowledge, we can move forward with purpose and confidence as we strive towards living our best lives. Ultimately, self-discovery is a journey of exploration and growth that can help us become the best version of ourselves.

Walking in your true authentic self allows your gift seed to flourish. Surrender to the undisputed origins of wince you came. Your unique upbringing and life experiences gives you the exclusive tool to display something no one else can. What if Steve Jobs never presented his ideas for the iPhone because he felt the idea was too radical?

Whenever we conform to a room to be more like the room, we are denying our unique gifts and talents the opportunity to expound and change the world. Can you imagine your life without the handheld computer knows as the iPhone? Android users...*shhhh*! Not knowing who you are will prevent you from making the correct decisions and choices. These decisions and choices will amplify your strengths, not what you think will be celebrated by society, friends, and family.

A few weeks ago, I busted into laughter after thinking how fragile I used to be in terms of criticism. If someone told me something I deemed negative about myself, it wasn't received well. While on my journey to becoming an author, I realized you have to survey feedback constantly. I had friends and family to review my book; no one instantly fell in love with the first draft. Then, I sent it to the editor for a less than stellar review. If I couldn't properly receive reviews from people I knew, how would I fare with complete strangers (no offense) reading my book and leaving reviews on Amazon? Would I abandon God's will or walk past the curses spewed with confidence that I know what God wants for my life.

Discover who you are so you can be the best version of you and share your strengths. When you don't know who you are, it's usually for one of two reasons:

...you've *suppressed* who you are.
...you're *ashamed* of who you are.

You've Suppressed Who You Are...

A major part of your self-discovery journey is becoming everything you want to be. Instead of doing the work to be the person we want others to perceive us to be, we may take the shortcut of suppressing who we are. When you suppress who you are, take on other identities of what you thought success looks like, and try to become a carbon copy of someone else, life becomes HARD. Imagine trying to study, read, and YouTube ways to garner the exact success of someone else. To do so, you would have to ignore the things you like, your instincts, your feelings, your thoughts, and attempt to do everything that person would do in the situations you face. This is not the blueprint.

I was in a similar position. I would think, "What would Jay-Z do?" I burst out in laughter writing this now, but I would really ask myself this question. I admired his bravado, his no-nonsense attitude, his passion when he explained things and persuaded people to act within his vision. But I'm not Jay-Z, Jigga, or Hov. I'm Brian Williams. I had to be intentional about recovering and revealing my true self. I was so suppressed and in bondage to an image of what I thought I needed to become successful. Being your authentic self takes bravery, freedom to fail, and commitment. Asking myself constantly who I am and what's important to me helped me overcome the bondage of people's perception of me. It also allowed me the freedom of knowing I am one of one.

Stop overthinking and just ACT...today! Tell yourself, "In the process of action, I will discover myself and what I'm good at." Once you know who you are, you will realize you are special enough to just be you. It's an amazing feeling that many can attempt to mimic but no one can be Brian D. Williams. One of my favorite actors growing up, Jim Carrey, said, "If you're not willing to downgrade your lifestyle for a year to have a lifestyle you want forever, you care too much what other people think." This relates to self-discovery in this way. If you are not willing to take a year to find out who you are and make a selection, you care about the wrong things.

You Are Ashamed of Who You Are

It's important to remember that there is purpose in who we are. We all have different strengths, weaknesses, and personalities—all of which play a role in how we learn and grow. If we try to be someone different than our true selves, it can fracture our confidence and hold us back from being the best version of ourselves. Keep in mind, no one is perfect, including you.

There is no reason to be ashamed of where you are currently. By being proud of our identity, we can use it as a tool for purposeful growth. Everyone has something unique to bring to the table. Being open and authentic about who you are makes it easier for others to understand and accept you. Don't be ashamed of who you are—you have purpose! Instead, embrace your identity and use it to create meaningful connections with others. Accepting who you are and being proud of your identity is one of the keys to living a purpose-filled life. It allows you to be open-minded and confident in yourself, allowing you to take risks, grow, and ultimately make an impact on the world.

Try saying daily affirmations in the mirror to increase your confidence. In the beginning it may feel silly; ultimately, you will begin to feel a shift. Don't let the fear of judgment or criticism keep you from being your true self. Embrace who you are and create a positive impact on the world around you.

Look For Strengths, Not Superpowers

An easier way to look at it would be to look for your strengths. Many look at the words 'gift' and 'talent' as superpowers. A strength is an easier way not to overlook something special you do that others find difficult. Can you win people over who you just met? Can you imagine things happening in the future and get people excited about them when they hear your explanation? Are you physically flexible? These are just a few strengths that can be developed as tools on your purpose journey.

Put yourself in position to use your strengths on a daily basis. There are many people currently working in fields that don't showcase their God-given talents. Maybe they work a certain job because their parents worked in that field. Maybe they chose a certain career because it pays a good salary. Chasing money or settling for a lineage track may not be aligned with your purpose. Work habits and industry knowledge can be passed down; but, not God-given talent. Michael Jordan was a great basketball player; some would say he was the best and I WOULD AGREE. If talent could be passed down, his son would have been a Hall of Famer as well. There's nothing regular about you if you are operating where God wants you to be. Look into your strengths and keep it in the forefront as you make your selection.

Selection

The action of choosing what you discover as one of your God-given talents is the selection process. A decisive moment must take place where you choose to act and take the intentional step towards your purpose. After reviewing the discovery list compiled in chapter 1, you will need to make a selection. Don't overthink this process. Make a selection and be decisive after prayer! Here's the good part, the only wrong selection you can make is not making a selection at all. Sometimes starting a task that you are semi interested in helps you discover what you like or dislike. So there's no way you could possibly waste time in your selection process unless you quit.

My selection process was done in true Brian Williams fashion. Over analyzing everything and needing confirmation from God in every step of the process.

Throughout my life, I was constantly shown and told that I have a natural talent for writing. In school, my English teachers complimented my passion for writing, and I won several awards. I've written over 100 songs just for the love of writing. I've been the family's document proofreader for as long as I can remember. I love coaching and helping people, so it would seem to not be a far stretch for me to write self-help books to help others. I especially like to use my trials as an example for all to learn from.

When making your selection, you will either be starting from ground zero or moving into an opportunity.

Ground Zero Selection: A ground zero selection is the starting point of pursuing a purpose act you have never tried before. You have been told you do something very well and should pursue it, but you have never invested time in that area. You have only chosen to invest your time in something that was comfortable, made sense financially, or an opportunity fell into your lap. A ground zero selection is an exciting journey but can be an overwhelming thought. Starting something new is not easy but we must remember we have to start somewhere. You are beginning with a blank canvas, and it's ok not to know how or what type of art you want to create. You are creating something that will withstand the test of time.

This type of selection also allows your family's lineage the opportunity to build from this selection for generations to come. I was just driving down the highway this morning and noticed so many company trucks that read 'a last name and sons.' James & Sons Plumbing, Smith & Sons Autos, Tim & Sons HVAC Repair, the list goes on and on. At some point, someone made a ground zero selection based off their God-given talents, and learned the skill set that they could teach their children. Have confidence that after isolating, reflecting, inventorying, and discovering, you are moving in the right direction. You were designed to complete something and now you are steps closer to that goal.

My last year of college, Walgreens was making a huge push to hire recent college graduates. They figured that recent college graduates were skilled enough to run their stores with little experience. The job market wasn't great in 2005. Without a great internship after graduating, one might find themselves struggling to find a new career. Regardless of your degree field, Walgreens hiring graduates was a well-known fact. Many graduates with education degrees, political science, mass communication, etc., took jobs with Walgreens. It made sense because no experience was required. This is an example of doing something comfortable that falls into your lap.

If you are not careful, you can find yourself 5 years into working a job that has nothing to do with your purpose but it was easy to obtain. While there is nothing wrong with working at Walgreens to make a decent paycheck, it's the reason behind the decision to make it a career that is questionable.

If you have kids, young siblings, or young family members, encourage them to do exploratory activities young before their income is a part of their survival. Make the decision to only walk in the direction of where your gift can be utilized to make the world a better place. A ground zero selection is the most difficult start but gives you the best return on investment. Mainly because there are no wasted steps. I have also witnessed colleagues work a job for income while working in their purpose. Exhausting as that may sound, actively working on something you are naturally talented in becomes easy and will create opportunities.

Moving into Opportunity: A moving into opportunity selection is using your current network and familiar territory to introduce yourself to your purpose. You may have worked at Coca-Cola for 10 years in marketing but recently discovered that because of your incredible attention to detail and natural disciplined mindset, you should apply for a position in the finance department. You are moving towards an opportunity in a familiar territory. An opportunity that, because it aligns with your core values, in a field you are naturally strong in, gives you fulfillment. Instead of starting over from ground zero you are using your current connections to move laterally or upwards.

Maybe you've been working in a field that you have zero

passion for but it's comfortable and pays well. You have learned how to do the job very well, but you don't enjoy doing it. Begin to reach out to your close resources such as people who attend your church, relatives, former classmates, and friends. Continue to pray daily for God to put you in the places that will allow your gift seed to grow. Keeping a clear and positive mindset and remaining open-minded will allow you to be ready when the opportunity presents itself.

Years ago my father started a business in the commercial janitorial industry. Before starting his business, he worked in janitorial services for over 20 years. It was an industry he was comfortable and confident he could perform well in. After graduating college, I accepted a position as a manager with Enterprise Rent-A-Car. Simultaneously, my father was struggling to retain clients because the services he offered were inconsistent. After concluding a call with him one evening where he sounded extremely exhausted from the day-to-day operations, I decided to take a leap of faith and help. I was frustrated with Enterprise Rent-A-Car's lack of opportunity for growth and decided to resign to assist my father's business in retaining current clients and encourage growth.

I went to college for marketing. Even though I was taking a pay decrease to leave Enterprise, I was excited to have the chance to use what I learned in marketing and business management. I have always been passionate about anything business related. I started small businesses as a youth and was able to do well. The move I made to my father's business, AccuClean, was moving into opportunity. I took a reduction in pay to select something that, after reflecting, realized I was passionate about. I have a talent of noticing the details to select the right employees. With that talent, I was able to select employees who could take the business to the next level. Using my gift of creating marketing plans for a specifically targeted group, I was able to double our client list.

Your purpose is how your unique gift is used in the world. Continue to be open-minded during this part of the process. After you make a decision, ask the Holy Ghost to affirm your talent or gift. The gift is buried inside of you in seed form. The easiest way to get to that would be self-discovery.

The Gift of Seed

Mark 4:26-33 is the parable of the growing seed. It states, "It is like a mustard seed, which, when it is sown on the ground, even though it is smaller than all the other seeds that are sown on the soil, Yet when it is sown, it grows up and becomes larger than all the garden herbs; and it puts out large branches. So that the birds of the sky are able to make nests and live under its shade."

Our purpose is a seed inside of us all. The verses just read are an example of how once sown and the soil takes to it, we are birthing a gift. Jesus chose to show parables using planting seeds for a reason.

Mark 13 discusses how at first some of the seeds that were spread on to the ground didn't make it to maturity. The reason is because they landed on hard, uncultivated walking paths. The ground was not prepared for seeds. Since the seeds were just laying on the ground, they awaited the fate of being eaten by the birds. Seeds that fall on walking pathways are like people who hear the word of God and the teachings of the Kingdom and just don't get it. Perhaps because their hearts are hardened or they are not prepared to receive the word. Then Satan comes in before the seeds can take root and swoops away just like a bird.

I had a very vivid dream on my purpose journey that spoke to me in such a profound way. This revelation was given to me by the Holy Spirit. I learn through analogies best because it's a comparison between two things usually to provide clarity by comparing something I'm already familiar with. There's nothing I know better than business and entrepreneurship.

I had a dream I was in a conference room setting with 20 people. The board chairman told all of us sitting at the conference table, "I'm going to gift you all a seed in soil in a flowerpot. You will not know what type of seed it is until it blossoms, but it will only blossom if it's taken care of properly. If you come back in a year's time with a healthy plant, I will invest in your seed company."

In business, a seed is an early-stage investment in a startup company, typically provided by angel investors or venture capitalists to help the company get off the ground. The investment is usually made in exchange for equity in the company. If you've ever watched the show "Shark Tank" it's a very similar process. The Sharks (investors) tell entrepreneurs, if you go along with the following guidelines, I will continue to invest in the seed until it's operating in the black above $1 million. Shortly after leaving the conference with a plant in my hand in my dream, I woke up.

The entire day I thought about that dream and what it meant. At the time, I was struggling with my identity and my purpose. I couldn't find the scripture that spoke to me to help me understand why I was here. When I got home later that evening, I started to research seeds. While there are a few definitions of the word seed, the one that resonated with me most is in botany. A seed is the reproductive structure of a flowering plant that contains an embryo and is capable of developing into a new plant. In my dream, I was told that if I properly took care of the seed, growing it into plant, I could come back for an investment in my company. I decided to study all I could about growing a plant. There were a couple things I noticed instantly.

- *Proper Spacing* - When planting seeds, you

shouldn't plant them too close together; crowding them will bother the natural germination process. I will cover this also, so you will not only find your purpose, you will also become a gardener, LOL. Crowded planting discourages growth, shade each other from the sun, and compete for water and soil nutrients. As this relates to finding your purpose, it means you must put yourself in a place where you have the opportunity to grow without interference, negative feedback, or a reason to compete with someone.

Isolating that seed so it can be allowed to grow properly over time is essential. I was guilty of being the person who shared my dreams with everyone. Today, I'm at the point where I only share my current ambitions with my loved ones once I have committed a certain amount of time to the task. Until you have allowed your dreams to grab root, allow yourself the proper spacing for the seed of purpose inside you.

- *Temperature* - When you are attempting to grow your seed, you must put it in the right environment and temperature. Certain plants only grow in the rainforest, deserts, or backyards in California. The seed must be in the right environment with the correct temperature to blossom and bear fruit. This part of the growth process of a seed relates to finding your purpose is the most experimental. You must be fearless to put your-self in places that may feel uncomfortable initially but allow you the opportunity to thrive. This is not a one size fits all. Everyone's purpose is differ-ent, we all thrive in different environments. To unlock our talents and gifts in purpose, we must be in the right place.

Check the temperature of the people you are surrounded by and spend the most time with. For every tree is known by his own fruit (Luke 6:43-45). Meaning if you want to know if you are spending time with the right group, check what's manifesting in their lives without judgment.

- *Oxygen* - There must be oxygen in the pores of the soil for seed growth to take place. If the seed is buried too deep in the soil, it will be deprived of proper oxygen. It is an important and essential source of energy required for seed growth. What are you equipping yourself with to grow inside? Educating yourself, engaging in self-help activi-ties, and reading the bible are ways to intake oxy-gen.

- *Water* - In the process of growing your seed, you must include water in the plans. Water initiates the process of imbibition. The water activates special proteins called enzymes that begin the process of seed growth. "I will send you rain in its season, and the ground will yield its crops and the trees their fruit," Leviticus 26:4 (NIV). This scripture explains that God will send the rain for your purpose seed to grow and yield crops. Have faith and spend time with Him in the word while preparing for this season. So when you receive your YES, you will be prepared to grow.

- *Protection of Seed in Infant Stages* - A common practice in farming is to put hay over areas spread with seeds. This keeps birds from eating the seeds before they take root and bring forth fruit. Also, constant heat from the sun can damage seeds. Covering the seeds with hay can help the ground retain moisture better, which improves germination.

  Whatever God has spoken to you is for you only until it takes root. If you are not careful, hearing doubt spoken from others can prevent you from doing the very thing God promised you.

  Protect your seed with hay in its infant stages. When I think about seed protection, I imagine how crazy people must have thought Steve Jobs or Jeff Bezos were. The idea of innovation is often thought of as radical or impossible until someone puts in the work to make it happen. Now, we live in a society where we can conveniently shop and have a package dropped at our front door, from a tap of a screen on a smartphone.

Proper spacing, temperature, oxygen, water, and protection all working together develop a plant of purpose. Your purpose selection should be treated as if you are nurturing a seed to a plant that will flourish and bear fruit.

Prayer:

Father God,

Me waking up this morning and drawing breath is a sign that you need me on this earth to fulfill your will.
Show me how my life can make this world a better place.
Show me how to make the correct purpose selection after traveling this road of self-discovery.
I'm willing to sacrifice my ego, pride, and plans for your plans.
Amen.

CHAPTER 3

○ ○ ○

Purpose on Hold

And let us not grow weary while doing good, for
in due season we shall reap if we do not
lose heart.

Galatians 6:9

The path to living a life of purpose is rarely a straight line. It's filled with twists, turns, and roadblocks. Whenever we choose a path that is met with resistance, we can become discouraged. These challenges are not signs that you're on the wrong path, but rather, opportunities for growth. Obstacles often serve as tests that refine our commitment to what matters most. Understanding these challenges—and knowing how to overcome them—can be the difference between staying stuck and moving forward with resilience.

In this chapter, we'll explore the most common internal and external barriers that can impede your progress, and I'll offer practical strategies for navigating through them. We'll also delve into how to reframe your mindset to see obstacles as steppingstones rather than roadblocks. It's okay for you to press pause on your purpose intentionally or unintentionally. However, learning what takes away your motivation to be a greater person is equally as important as the pursuit of purpose itself.

Overcoming obstacles is a crucial part of the journey to living a life of purpose. Each challenge, whether internal or external, presents a chance to strengthen your commitment, learn new skills, and grow as a person. Remember, obstacles do not define your ability to achieve your purpose—they simply test how much you're willing to pursue it. By embracing these challenges with resilience, self-compassion, and strategic thinking, you can turn them into steppingstones toward a more meaningful and fulfilling life. While on this journey, life will continue to happen. It is important to remain steadfast in the direction of what you are trying to accomplish.

Once you discover your purpose, you can unintentionally put it on hold. It can be exciting in the beginning. Finally, you are aware of the few things that you do extremely well! Suddenly, something happens which may cause you to lose focus on your purpose. You may feel attacked reading this chapter. Hang in there champ, it gets better.

I lost my drive and motivation to operate in my purpose a few times and didn't know it was even possible to regain it. A constant part of life we all know is that there will be ups and downs. God never promised that our lives would be perfect. He said He would be with us and never leave us during trying times.

In our lowest moments, we may lose sight or forget our purpose. One of the biggest lies Satan told me, and many others, is that MY sin was so great God no longer favors me. Believing that deception will switch something inside of you so you no longer seek God's guidance because you view Him as not being in your corner. He will never leave you or forsake you. I don't believe there's anything my kids can do to stop me from loving them. God feels the same way, we are His children. Whenever you feel like God isn't there, remember the teacher is always quiet during the test.

No one who's known me for the last 20 years would believe I'm writing a spiritual self-help book. I've had some very dark moments that I was able to conceal from the public. The only way to find the motivation you've lost is to start back seeking. It all begins with the first step. Let's take it back to the beginning when you were excited about that new job, marriage, volunteer work, or hobby. Revisit the beginning and we can figure out exactly where we derailed. There's no step more important than the first one. Some of society's most revered people are individuals who weren't afraid of failing, learning from their mistakes, and starting over again.

This chapter is dedicated to the person very familiar with what their talents and gifts are but continue to allow life's moments to derail them from what they truly deserve. What was promised to them through scripture is still available today.

There are different obstacles that can stand in our way in our purpose journey. Looking at these obstacles as opportunities to improve ourselves allows us the grace to continue to chase our dreams. The obstacles are in three different categories: external, emotional, and internal.

External obstacles can be defined as your current life circumstances and setbacks. External obstacles arise from your environment or circumstances. This can include financial constraints with a tight budget, time limitations from leading a large family, responsibilities for taking care of an aging parent, or just a lack of support from others. Sometimes, these obstacles seem beyond your control. These challenges, though real, can be approached strategically. By identifying what's within your control, you can create solutions that allow you to adapt and keep moving forward. There will never be a perfect, opportune time to work on yourself. It takes practice for you to carve out time to focus on your goals. Others may see it as being selfish in the beginning and may become upset with you. In time, they will understand.

Emotional obstacles can be defined as a fear of change and uncertainty. Change is inherently uncomfortable, especially when it involves stepping into new territory. Even when a change is positive, the uncertainty it brings can trigger fear and anxiety. Then, fear can manifest into FSJ! Fear of failure, fear of success, and fear of judgment.

Fear of failure is the worry that trying something new might lead to a negative outcome. The truth is, we will never know anything if we don't give it a try. Fear of success can be daunting for some. Like. *What if this really works and gives me new responsibilities I'm not ready for? Maybe I should just keep doing what I'm comfortable with.* Don't lose your motivation to try something new. Lean in and discover what success feels like.

Fear of judgment is the fear of how others will perceive your choices or changes in your life. These fears can keep you from taking necessary steps toward your purpose, leading to procrastination or hesitation. By understanding their origins, you can learn to manage them effectively.

Internal obstacles are defined by limiting beliefs within your mind. The first step to overcoming limiting beliefs is identifying them. What thoughts arise when you think about pursuing your purpose? What are the doubts and fears that surface? Once you've identified these thoughts, challenge their validity. Ask yourself, "Is this absolutely true?" Often, you'll find these thoughts are based on fear rather than facts; things deeply rooted in your mind from past experiences that have created imaginary barriers and obstacles. For example, if you think, "I'm not talented enough," look for evidence that contradicts this belief. Reflect on past achievements or moments when you've excelled in a skill. Then, replace the limiting belief with an empowering one, such as, "I have unique talents that the world needs."

Reasons We Lose the Identity of Purpose...

Life will always come at you relentlessly. One of the reasons we lose the identity of our purpose is because we can't see instant progress. There are steps involved in completing any long-term goals. Meaning, to accomplish the goals, we must complete a process.

I'm currently the president of a multi-million-dollar janitorial service in Atlanta, GA. The business was started on an opportunity that was given to my father by someone willing to offer tutelage on how to properly run a cleaning service. Seeing how impactful that experience was for my father, I pay-it-forward by mentoring almost anyone who's interested in getting into the industry. Many of the business owners I've sat down with for free business coaching in my industry lose focus. We have discussed marketing plans that can help them grow their business, and the owners quit them in 30 days.

I ask, "What type of marketing did you do?"

"Brian, I sent out 500 postcards, and no one called to book my pressure washing services! Maybe this isn't where God wants me to be."

Once you have committed an action to a decision you have made, allow the decision an opportunity to show you if it's going to work. In this microwave society, it's very easy to become distracted. If you have a Tik Tok account and scrolled on it for 20 minutes, you have been exposed to more than most can process within an hour. Write down what you decide to do, commit unwavering action towards it, and watch your action work.

Satan heard you voice indecisiveness out loud. Soon after, doubt and fear of failure appear on our bookshelf. Yup! Everyone has a bookshelf they leave their dreams on when the task becomes too daunting. We leave dreams there and say we'll come back to them. We forget all about them, then ask God to reveal our purpose.

Dust your dream off and get back to it. Most consumers need to see an ad 7-8 times before the call-to-action clicks. This is the same process with your purpose. It takes visiting our purpose a few times before realizing this is what we were called to do. If God has placed it on your heart to do a podcast, do it! Your first episode may only have two views. That's ok. Have faith in your purpose. You are the righteousness of God! You can do this! It's a recipe. A relationship with God first, a bit of work stamina, a dash of faith, and *voila*! Your podcast starts doing numbers. Don't forget who you are and what you are capable of.

Record Your Start...

Keep the same energy you had in the beginning. Don't wait until you achieve your goal to be proud of yourself for starting. Ways to maintain the excitement you get when starting the new journey to purpose are to start a journal, blog, or vlog. There will be times when you question the reason you started. You can easily refer back to the way you captured your original intentions. You can get to a point where there's so much resistance that you question everything. Who can better motivate you than an excited, passionate, past version of YOU?

I've started business ventures that I looked back on 2 or 3 years later and had no idea why I decided to involve myself. After I began regularly recording myself to capture moments, I reflected back to one opportunity only because it had high profit margins. I spent countless hours doing something I did not enjoy hoping it would yield a large revenue of income. As I reached back to get that initial passion I felt when starting, it was revealed I began for the wrong reasons. I gained clarity to then make the right decision in the current day.

If it was up to my natural ambition, I wouldn't get much done. I imagine it like a yellow brick road with a sign every half a mile that says, "You are almost there, keep going!" There's a logical explanation to why God gives you the vision but doesn't explain the road to the vision and how to make it happen. If most of us knew there would be a lot of hungry nights, long studying hours, cramming for finals, and financial challenges, we would've never applied for college. The process was a mixture of lessons, struggles, and lifelong bonds that can never be replaced. The road was challenging but worth every moment experienced.

Some journal entries I review years later, I'm amazed at how far I've come and the things I've accomplished that God brought me through. We all often forget our successes but write our failures in stone. Imagine you've spent years excelling in your career, receiving awards for your leadership and innovation. People praised your dedication and called you a role model. Then, one year, you make a poor investment decision that costs your company significant money.

Suddenly, the accolades fade, and the narrative shifts. It feels as if your years of achievement have been erased, while the failure is etched permanently in people's minds, overshadowing everything else. Society often magnifies failures while diminishing the significance of long-standing accomplishments. Record your wins, not just your losses.

Here's an experiment. Journal to a future version of yourself 3 years into the future. What would you tell the 2028 you? What are some challenges you would like to overcome? What would you like your family to look like? Your bank account?

Amazingly, the Holy Spirit speaks to me whenever I journal telling me ways to get started on what I'm journaling. Writing down your prayers and goals unlocks so many things in your life that you simply must act on daily. Spending this type of time daily developing yourself is essential.

Your Vision is For You Only...

God only reveals the vision of your life to you. So many people's confidence is destroyed by loved ones, family, or friends. Again, they can't figure this out for you or even give you advice. Especially if it leads with, "You got to hustle or grind it out." What does that even mean? Pray, read, and talk to God.

Be very careful with who you reveal your purpose to in the fetal stages of your process. Allow the purpose to grow and grab hold of you and gain confidence in fulfillment of what you are doing. As said in the previous chapter allow your seed it's proper spacing. Because your vision was not shown to your friends, spouse, or family, they may not be able to visualize the same fruition as you. So, intentionally or unintentionally, they can speak doubt and fear to the purpose you pursue to operate in. The intention of their feedback, whether solicited or unsolicited, is not important. Depending on how well-rooted you are in the process, their feedback can derail your train to purpose.

Jay-Z often references an uncle he told about his dreams of becoming a rap superstar and selling a million records. His uncle quickly debunked his dream stating he would never sell a million records. Now Jay-Z says he sold a million records like a million times. Someone else's opinion can't hold mental real estate that allows you to question the very thing God placed on your heart. If you are not careful, receiving negative feedback is one of the ways we place our purpose on hold after discovering it.

I could never fix my mouth to say or my pen to write that you are lazy because you are not operating in your purpose or unaware of your God-given gifts. No matter your age or background, God can use your story for His glory.

It's easy to tell someone they need to get up early and figure it out but that's incorrect. While it will take effort, you are primarily still in your circus because of a lack of knowledge. You don't know what to do, so either you do all the wrong things or your minimal positive progress is untraceable. You've made a huge step in the right direction by reading this book and gaining knowledge on how to operate.

As you walk on the journey of discovering your purpose, I want to reveal the obstacles that can hinder your progress. At one time, I thought the statement, "All the answers are in the Bible," was exaggerated. I questioned how this ancient book could teach me to become a successful entrepreneur in 2025. Here's the truth no one ever told me: the Bible holds countless treasures of wisdom.

Reading it not only draws you closer to God but also transforms and renews your mind. It teaches you how to live a purposeful life and fosters a deep relationship with Him and the Holy Spirit. This connection becomes your spiritual GPS, guiding your steps and helping you discern which moves to make—or avoid. You no longer have to rely solely on your own understanding, a burdensome and exhausting task. Instead, you can navigate life with confidence, knowing you're connected to a higher source of wisdom.

Telling Yourself You Don't Have Time...

You go to work, you make sure your spouse or significant other is happy, you take care of the kids, the dog, hang with friends, check on your parents, clean the house... I can keep going, but I'll stop there. Being too busy to work on your purpose goals means you lack focus, not time. With this thought process, you can unintentionally put your purpose on hold.

You are in control of your time. Prepare to win and if not...you're preparing to fail. Set aside the time in isolation to hear from God. On your way to work or school, sit in silence and ask the Holy Spirit to reveal your gifts to you. I am now intentional about the time I spend with God. I want to know Him better, not just for what he can do for me, but because I appreciate everything he has already done. Life is easier with him as the coach. Instead of spending a lifetime trying to figure things out, I just ask Him for revelation.

My time management mindset changed when I began to view it in terms of currency. Every day we get a $1,440 direct deposit in minutes, but we HAVE TO SPEND IT. For a week I wrote down what I spent my money on. The things I viewed as wasteful or excessive, I cut back on. Netflix, Falcons football (my most toxic relationship), social media (your bad experience at Walmart-mart today served me no purpose), and listening to sport shows were just a few things I could cancel out or cut back on. For some reason, going to the bathroom or eating by myself were my most wasteful moments. I started reading scriptures about time management and felt led to manage my time better.

Proverbs 21:5 says "The plans of the diligent lead only to plenty, but everyone who is hasty comes only to poverty." Productivity went through the roof! Before writing this book, I would only read one book every couple of years. Can you believe that? It would take me years to read something that would make me a better person. Now, I won't go a day without reading a chapter. Renew your mind, and you'll find the time #BARS.

Story of Jairus...

There's a story in the Bible that perfectly puts the proper perspective of not giving up or losing motivation on God's promises. In Luke chapter 8, Jairus has a daughter who is very ill. When Jesus comes into town, Jairus goes looking for Jesus to heal his daughter. While Jairus was waiting to get Jesus' attention, someone relayed the message of his daughter's passing and asked for him to leave the teacher alone. This suggests that the person who told Jairus she died believed there was nothing Jesus could do. They probably believed Jesus could only heal the sick, not revive the dead. There is no dedicated verse to support this, but I believe Jesus knew this was happening in the midst of healing someone else.

Even though Jairus was told that his daughter was

already dead, Jairus didn't give up. Jesus knew what Jairus was feeling and asked him to believe. Jairus believed because he continued with Jesus and followed Him into the house. When Jesus entered, He told the people the girl was sleeping. Jesus knew He was about to wake her up. Jesus said, "Little girl get up." She instantly awakened, healed and restored.

It's easy for us to lose motivation on what God has promised when we face even just one thing that suggests the opposite. What was the one thing you stopped doing because you felt it was unrecoverable? What dream or goal did you stop pursuing because you felt like it was dead?

Today, I'm asking you to wait for Jesus to tell that thing to get up! Your promise is still here, God is going to deliver it. Don't be discouraged with the timetable. The process is not to delay you or deny you but to develop you. Not to put a hold or a pause on what you want to become but to prepare you for your next season. STAY MOTIVATED.

CHAPTER 4
○ ○ ○
Satan's Trick

The gift of God is irrevocable.

Romans 11:29

This chapter's scripture is a part of the larger context of Romans 11, where the Apostle Paul discusses God's plan for Israel and the Gentiles. In Romans 11:29, Paul emphasizes the unchanging nature of God's gifts and calling. The idea is that once God bestows His gifts or calls someone to a particular purpose, He does not change His mind or take back those gifts. This verse underscores the faithfulness and reliability of God's promises.

Satan wants you to turn from God in the midst of your suffering. Satan is after your prayer life and to keep you from praying, he provides many things to distract you. He wants you to shut down your communication with God and depend only on yourself. Satan's tool has been deceit since the beginning. If we are unaware of the tactics he employs, we can find ourselves in positions of believing things that prevent us from operating in our purpose.

In the culture of today's society the word "receipts" has been popularized to mean "proof." It's important to do the work in the previous chapters to get your receipts so there's no doubt in the places you need to operate in. God's plan for you is always better than your plan. However, by living a life of fear, regret, and self-doubt, you will never reach that designed potential.

In football, any coach worth his salt is going to study a ton of film on the upcoming opponent. The coaches will research the best players on the opposing team, the plays they like to run, and the style of plays likely to be called. (In my DJ Khalid voice). There's no way possible for me to write a book about purpose without devoting a chapter to the opposing head coach who doesn't want you to win. Satan is not very creative, in fact the same three ways Satan tried to trick Jesus in the desert are the ways he will try to prevent you from opening your gift and figuring out your purpose.

The devil knows he can't stop you from reaching heaven—Jesus secured that for you through His sacrifice. All you need to do is accept what Jesus has done. Still, the devil will attempt to make your life horrible here on Earth. His main focus is to make sure you don't reach your potential. There are three ways he can keep you from your potential. These are the same three ways he tempted Jesus in the desert. Before Jesus started his ministry and decided to walk in His purpose in the book of Matthew in the New Testament, Jesus fasted.

Physical Temptation:
Doing what feels right (Matthew 4:3-4)
Jesus was out in the desert fasting for 40 days with no food or water. Satan tried to appeal to the flesh of Jesus saying if you are who you think you are, turn these stones into bread so you can eat it.

Your feelings can be deceiving. Just because something feels right doesn't mean you should indulge. Jesus was able to overcome this temptation by saying 'man doesn't live on bread alone but the word of God.' I'm sure Jesus was tempted but with the word, He was able to resist for a great purpose. When you are feeling that your physical flesh is being tempted to act in accordance with what doesn't align with your purpose, protect yourself by doing the following:

Scripture: Romans 12:2 (NIV) - "Do not conform to the pattern of this world but be transformed by the renewing of your mind. Then you will be able to test and approve what God's will is—his good, pleasing and perfect will."
Principle: Regularly engage with Scripture and prayer to align your thoughts and desires with God's will. By doing this you **RENEW YOUR MIND.**

Scripture: Proverbs 4:23 (NIV) - "Above all else, guard your heart, for everything you do flows from it."
Principle: Be mindful of the influences and desires that can lead you into temptation. Guard your heart and focus on things that align with God's teachings. By doing this you **GUARD YOUR HEART.**

Scripture: 1 Corinthians 6:18 (NIV) - "Flee from sexual immorality. All other sins a person commits are outside the body, but whoever sins sexually, sins against their own body."
Principle: Instead of trying to confront or rationalize

with temptation, remove yourself from situations that may lead to physical temptations. **FLEE TEMPTATION** at all costs.

Scripture: James 5:16 (NIV) - "Therefore confess your sins to each other and pray for each other so that you may be healed. The prayer of a righteous person is powerful and effective."

Principle: Have accountability partners within your faith community with whom you can share your struggles, and seek support and prayer. Hold each other **ACCOUNTABLE.**

Scripture: Matthew 26:41 (NIV) - "Watch and pray so that you will not fall into temptation. The spirit is willing, but the flesh is weak."

Principle: Pray for strength, wisdom, and guidance to resist temptation. Cultivate a consistent prayer life. **PRAY** daily.

Scripture: Psalm 101:3 (NIV) - "I will not look with approval on anything that is vile. I hate what faithless people do; I will have no part in it."

Principle: Be cautious about the media and entertainment you consume. Choose content that aligns with biblical values. **BE MINDFUL** of entertainment.

Scripture: Hebrews 13:4 (NIV) - "Marriage should be honored by all, and the marriage bed kept pure, for God will judge the adulterer and all the sexually immoral."

Principle: If married, prioritize the sanctity of your marriage and remain faithful to your spouse. The **COVENANT IN MARRIAGE** is important.

Scripture: Philippians 4:13 (NIV) - "I can do all this through him who gives me strength."

Principle: Rely on God's strength to overcome temptations. Pray for guidance and the power to resist. **SEEK GOD'S STRENGTH**.

Emotional Temptation:
Questioning God's love (Matthew 4:5-7)

In this verse, the devil took Jesus to the highest point of the temple in Jerusalem and said, "If you are the Son of God, jump off! For the scriptures say, He will order his angels to protect you. And they will hold you up with their hands so you won't even hurt your foot on a stone." The devil was trying to get Jesus to test God's love for him.

If you allow the untruths to manifest in your heart, you will require things that God has already promised you to be proven. Why must God constantly show you things to be true? His words are sufficient. Jesus responded to the devil, "The scriptures also say, 'You must not test the Lord your God.'" Don't allow your emotions to sway what God has already promised. The seed within you can't be changed by Satan. Remain disciplined and non-wavering in God's promises. Cultivate the fruit of the Spirit, which includes self-control. Seek God's help in managing your emotions and responding in a manner that aligns with His teachings. Develop a habit of gratitude. Focus on the positive aspects of life, acknowledge God's blessings, even in challenging situations. Be mindful of the thoughts and emotions you allow into your heart. Guard against negative influences and focus on God's truth. Equipping yourself with the knowledge necessary to win in the fight of emotions.

Control Temptation:
Take over the throne (Matthew 4:8-10)
Next, the devil took Him to the peak of a very high mountain and showed Him all the kingdoms of the world and their glory. "I will give it all to you," he said. "If you will kneel down and worship me." The control temptation runs rampant in today's society.

The devil was having his way with Earth. Jesus' purpose was to come to establish God's Kingdom. The devil was offering a shortcut to control and power. Jesus knew what was required to fulfill His purpose with God. The devil offered that if Jesus would kneel down and worship, he wouldn't have to go through the pain of the cross. The devil was essentially saying, you can have control on your own terms and in your own way without the pain.

Jesus didn't want to go to the cross in his flesh, but he knew he had to. "Get out of here, Satan," Jesus told him. For the Scriptures say, "You must worship the Lord your God and serve only him." That's why I'm so thankful for what Jesus did for me. And when offered a shortcut to power, Jesus declined the offer for my salvation.

In our lives, we have the temptation to do things our way, not God's way. Many times I have self-educated to the point of being defiant in the mission I was told to complete. Whether for money or pride, I can not serve God and mammon. I wouldn't allow God to steer my life even though He is all knowing. I wanted to have control and power to hurry the process of my success. I broke the spirit of mammon by trusting God more than I trust money. Giving all of the control to God and believing in Him aligns us with being in the right environment for our inner purpose seeds to flourish.

Beat Your Goals Up, Not Yourself

There are many people who went to the graveyard with their gifts still in inside them in seed form. Their gifts never grew because what those individuals told themselves prevented the seeds from blossoming. No one speaks to you more than you. What you tell yourself can be uplifting or damaging.

So what does beating yourself up look like? The easiest way to define this is the act of criticizing or questioning yourself about something that happened in the past or hasn't happened at all. So many let the chance that our fears could materialize keep us from even attempting to complete the task. A close relationship with God releases you from the shackles of guilt. Receive the gift of salvation and accept what Jesus has done for you. He knew we weren't capable of being perfect, so why beat yourself up when you come up short? We can continue moving forward in the direction we are destined for because he walks with us.

Doing the work to know the special seed of purpose inside of you will prevent you from giving space to things that haven't happened. I can count on many occasions where I was overthinking scenarios and wouldn't try because of fear of rejection. In my current alignment with God, I don't fear any opportunity, and I'm not afraid to try new things to further myself. My prayer is for me to only receive the things I need to honor Him and further my family.

Those who beat themselves up speak negative thoughts over themselves in a way they would never speak to others. It's very difficult to see any progress in life when you are losing the war in your mind. When negative thoughts overpower the positive, it can be draining. Practice mental exercises on the draining days. When you think a negative thought, follow it up with a positive thought immediately.

Treat yourself with kindness, challenge your negative thoughts with the word of God, and let go of guilt. Understand that holding onto guilt and shame is counter-productive. Forgive yourself for past mistakes, knowing that everyone makes errors. The enemy would like nothing more than to have you remain your own worst enemy. Write down a list of goals you want to accomplish and beat that list, not yourself!

Outside Influences

Don't allow outside influences of other people's frustrations to cause you to miss your purpose and calling. There was a portion of Moses' story where he disobeyed God because of the negative influence of the Israelites he'd just aided in rescue. The promise was the entry to the promised land. The Israelites grew frustrated with how long the travel was and began to lean into Moses' ear with negativity. There was so much disobedience that the promise was removed from Moses and the children of Israel.

Some people are simply not equipped for the next chapter of your life and don't see what God placed only in your vision. If you planned a 5-day vacation to Bora Bora but people voiced their opinion that you shouldn't go because they heard it was an unhealthy place, would you still go? If we are not careful, we can allow people to keep us away from something God has promised us because of myths and misinformation.

Myths About Finding Purpose

There are numerous misconceptions surrounding what it means to discover and live life with purpose, leading some astray on their quest. Let's clear up these misperceptions as they can act as roadblocks on your quest towards living more fulfilling lives.

Myth 1

Your Purpose Should Be Grand or World-Changing

A common misconception is that one's purpose must be something grandiose, such as curing disease or starting a global movement. This belief might make the pursuit of purpose seem out of reach for those of us not reaching such lofty heights. In truth, purpose can be found through everyday acts of love and service, such as raising children with love or teaching in ways which spark their curiosity; even being supportive friends helps others feel seen and heard. The enemy would like for you to believe the task is so grand and out of reach that you won't even start it. Or if you do attempt to start and come up short, that you will never try it again. Purpose doesn't need to be grandiose, it just has to be something meaningful to you.

Myth 2

You Only Have One Purpose

Another pervasive myth is the belief that every

individual possesses only a singular, unchanging purpose that they need to discover. This can create unnecessary pressure for finding "the" right thing immediately. In reality, your purpose may change over time as your interests shift or your circumstances alter. We are all very complex beings with different experiences and upbringings.

At first, your purpose may lie in providing support to a loved one during an emotionally trying time. As time progresses, it could evolve to advocating for others or finding creative ways to support your community. Don't feel bad if your purpose changes over time. What matters is that it aligns with your values and stage in life.

Myth 3
Once You Discover Your Purpose, Everything Will Fall Into Place

It's easy to assume that once you discover your purpose, everything will fall into place with ease and there won't be any more uncertainty in your journey. But even on paths which seem meaningful, there can still be hurdles ahead – you may question your direction, experience setbacks or struggle with self-doubt. You must continue to remind yourself who you are in the kingdom.

Purpose isn't about eliminating uncertainty; rather, it's about finding motivation to continue moving forward when things become uncertain. A sense of purpose provides a lighthouse during stormy conditions, helping us navigate safely through them while not smoothing them over completely.

You will have to battle physical temptation, emotional temptation, and control temptation. Staying aware of these temptations can help you avoid falling victim. Encourage yourself by remaining positive and focusing on fruitful outcomes. The wrong outside influences can drown out the only voice you should be focusing on. Dispel myths and work diligently towards being the person you aspire to be.

He who loves pleasure will become a poor man;
He who loves wine and oil will not become rich.

Proverbs 21:17

E very day we flip a coin, whether we are aware of it or not. We choose between operating in our purpose or doing things that give us pleasure. Take some time to journal what you did yesterday. Next to each task, write down whether it was for pleasure or purpose. The way to differentiate between the two is to ask yourself if the task you did is going to put you closer to the will of God and fulfill your purpose or something you did purely to relax or bring yourself some form of enjoyment?

When I choose purpose, I slowly walk into the task, gain momentum, and feel great after I complete it. When I choose pleasure, I happily walk into it, enjoy myself most times, and feel as if I could've used my time more wisely. This will be different for everyone but it's important to figure out your style to provide balance.

I have friends who have no problem working 12-14 hour days and vacationing twice a year for balance. At the same time, I also have friends who do the bare minimum in their careers and go on vacations once a month. Once you have determined your style, find an accountability partner who you can be transparent with to hold you in balance.

The things I enjoyed doing 3 months ago, I don't remember. The reason I don't remember is because the act of pleasure is temporary, equivalent to writing in the sand at the shore of a beach. For example, going on a vacation is not a long-term feeling. It's a temporary break from your normal life routine. Completing school or attending a webinar on financial peace is an example of a purpose act. A purpose act is one that doesn't give you anything immediate but allows you to better position yourself to reach your purpose. It can also be added to your tool belt of things to use again throughout your lifetime. Something that you can teach your lineage, so they won't have to learn it through life's toughest professor...Dr. Experience.

Attaining pleasure does not automatically equal happiness. We can often chase things that give us pleasure but the things that provide the most fulfillment you can't do in one day. So we are faced with the decision of doing temporary things to feel good daily or making purposeful decisions that make us feel more fulfilled operating in our purpose. It's important to be able to first distinguish the difference between the two on a daily basis. What's the difference between a purposeful day and a pleasurable day.

Purpose Day

A purpose day is a day where you focus on operating in your purpose. Since you've already put in the work to select your purpose, start off being prepared to execute what you would like to achieve that day. First, you need a healthy day of planning and a good night's rest. I highly recommend sitting down and jotting your thoughts, what would you like to accomplish, and what you need to make it happen.

Now that you have clearly defined what is needed in order to successfully complete your day, you have to execute the day. Throughout the day you may receive distractions that will attempt to derail your progress. I received three phone calls while writing this and decided to finish it, so I'm speaking from experience! Since you have planned how this day will go, try your very best to complete the things you set out to complete.

A chair is designed with a purpose to hold you when you sit on it. It is designed to withstand the weight of your body and keep you in a position until you decide to get up. Look at your day the same way. Once planned, it's designed to contribute to your God-given purpose. I may not remember August 16, 2023, but on this day, I completed a chapter in a book that was designed to inspire people all over the world to leave their chaotic lifestyle of pleasure to find purpose. Just the thought of you being intentional on carving out the time for your purpose makes it a purpose day. How effective you are at checking tasks off on your purpose day depends solely on you.

I recently shared this concept with my men's group, Men of Wisdom. After 30 days, we met again to share our experience with designed purpose days. We all agreed that the sense of fulfillment you receive after checking off the task list is beyond belief. There can be some forms of pleasure in your day but completing what you planned to do is the most important. I am reaping the harvest of seeds I planted years ago. Please review the purpose day template I have provided below to accelerate your progress in achieving your goals.

1. *(Prayer)* Starting the day off with prayer is a way to express gratitude for blessings, both big and small. Let God know you acknowledge and appreciate the blessings He has provided. Also, seeking forgiveness for mistakes you made and acknowledges what you did wrong while striving for personal improvement. Your spiritual connection is important, as you have no idea what the day may hold, but He does! Having Him there to guide you is paramount.

2. *(Exercise)* Relieve the stress you may have knowingly or unknowingly by setting up a good 30-minute exercise routine. This could be something you do at home or at a gym. I also utilize the time on the treadmill to review the tasks I must complete each day and what it would take to complete them.

3. *(Notate)* Write down the tasks you need to complete that will help you get out of the circus and closer to your purpose. No more than five tasks should be listed. It's important for them to be done with quality and accuracy.

4. *(Make a Living)* If you are scheduled to work

today, do what's necessary to secure your income.

5. *(Review)* As the day nears its close, you must now determine how productive your purpose day really was. If there are some tasks that need to be completed and you have the time to complete them, 'just do it' like Nike. If they can't be completed today, roll them over to the next day. Another reason I recommend your task list doesn't have more than five tasks, is to decrease the chances of the rollover list being more than five daily.

6. *(Rollover)* Write down the task(s) you couldn't complete and why you believe you were unable to complete them. Review the reasons you were unable to complete the task(s).

Pleasure Day

Pleasure days should be designed to provide balance. You could be feeling exhausted and need a break from the hustle and bustle of concurrent purposeful days. A pleasure day can restore you from physical exhaustion, anxiety, mental stress and overload. Maybe you have been overworking yourself and need to establish some balance.

Pleasure days start off led by emotion. It all depends on how you feel. What can you plan to do today that will make you happy? It can be a day filled with shopping or sightseeing. Hanging with friends and attending sporting events. Maybe even binge watching your favorite show on Netflix in bed. YOU SHOULD NOT FEEL BAD FOR PLEASURE DAYS. You just can't have too many of them. A pleasure day can be used as a recharge to fuel yourself towards your purpose the next day. Set a comfortable and calm ambiance in your environment, with lowlights, natural sounds or soothing music, and comfortable temperatures. Practice mindfulness and focus on being present in the moment to fully enjoy and appreciate your surroundings and activities.

I'm guilty of feeling bad for taking a break from pursuing my dreams. The truth is if I'm using time management properly, I will progressively get to my goals. But how good would my product of being a writer be if I'm always writing from a place of exhaustion and discomfort? My grandmother would always say the sun shines for a reason and the clouds rain for a reason. This easily applies to pleasure versus purpose. You have to view it as an age-old battle that must be attended to. As earlier stated, do not allow it to be one of Satan's tricks to derail you.

Have you ever heard of writer's block? It's when you reach a point in writing where creativity is low and you struggle to formulate complete thoughts or write productively. It is suggested that the way to cure writer's block is to step away and do something you enjoy or find pleasure in. Allowing yourself time to stop thinking and detach from writing refreshes you. This applies identically to your purpose balance. Allow time to experience some relief, refuel, and drive towards your purpose.

I was raised in a culture of working 5 days a week and doing what I want to do on the 2 weekend days. There's some balance with this approach. You may need to use the days you are off to regain focus. Now with the freshest version of yourself, you can reach new heights.

Instant Gratification

Have you ever felt like you heard your phone ring or felt a vibration only to pull out your phone and see no notifications? Studies show this can be a sign of unhealthy usage of our mobile devices. We are currently living in an era where many people show everyone what they are doing on social media. One of the reasons they do this is to receive instant gratification. Being able to receive something instantly isn't always bad. In the world of Uber, DoorDash, Amazon, and Instacart, we are able to get things faster at the touch of a phone.

Instant gratification is the desire to satisfy a craving immediately. Instant pleasure could be someone booking a trip and flying out to a beach that week, yet spending the money to upstart a business may not be as glamorous or something you'd want to capture and share instantly for gratification. Daily, we are faced with the decision to choose between pleasure or purpose. Don't make the mistake of always choosing what's fun today and doesn't contribute to your legacy.

Famous author, Heather King was quoted saying, "The irony of instant gratification is that it leaves such lasting scars." I believe this quote implies that even though you are receiving something instantly, it's leaving a lasting impression on who you are personally. If you are receiving everything instantly, it changes your approach to reach meaningful goals. Imagine getting your coffee and breakfast from an app, catching an uber to work, voice texting your work assignment, scheduling your lawn care on an app, and then your boss asks for you to prepare to lead a presentation tomorrow.

Your impulsive thought may first be to pay someone else to do it or go to ChatGPT. The proper time needed to make sure this presentation goes without a hitch would be at least 4-6 hours to create and proofread it. But all day you have completed numerous tasks with the click of a button.

Growing up as a millennial, this is a challenge I face too often for my liking. God may have placed something on your heart to complete that may take years. If God told us how long some of our purpose acts would take, most of us would never start. Patience is a good quality to have in the kingdom.

Delayed Gratification

Most of life's measurable moments will be an accumulation of good decisions made daily. And this process is called delayed gratification. My generation of millennials hate delayed gratification. We want to know everything instantly and lose motivation on the things in our lives that don't offer it.

Delayed gratification refers to the ability to resist the temptation of an immediate reward in favor of a larger or more long-term reward. It is often considered a key component of self-control and a predicator of success in areas such as academics, career, and financial stability. Studies have shown that individuals who are able to delay gratification tend to have better social and emotional well-being, as well as better physical health. Techniques such as mindfulness and setting specific goals can help individuals develop the ability to delay gratification. Why is this important in terms of discovering what your purpose is?

Simple. You have to be patient and disciplined in this process. There are so many examples from successful pastors who preached to a congregation of 10 people for several years until their message was able to reach the masses. Being okay with delayed gratification allows time for the seed inside of you to develop. Nothing great grows overnight. It allows you time to become great at whatever you are starting. Even though we start things we are naturally passionate about in our purpose journey, we may not be great at them in the beginning. Lower your expectations to not expect instant praise for your new venture.

Many of us come up with great ideas and things we can do with our talents and gifts but lack the discipline to focus long enough to give birth to it. We yield to the devil's distractions, indulging in pleasure instead of operating in purpose. God's plans for us are so great the enemy has to present a distraction to prevent you from seeing them.

Everyone can be great. Greatness is not limited to a certain number of people. Everyone can be great! In the past, whenever I heard, "God has great plans for you," I instantly downplayed it. I wondered how was it possible that everyone had a great destiny? Yet everyone does, some just choose pleasure daily.

Your obedience will be rewarded. 1 Samuel 15:22 says when God speaks to you and asks you to do something, do it. Everyone can think of that one relationship where you felt your advice wasn't being listened to. At some point, you may stop advising, feeling it's falling on deaf ears. My oldest daughter is the perfect example. In some of our 'adulting" conversations, she leads with emotion because she doesn't want to go through any discomfort even if it's for her own benefit in the long run. It's easier for me to see the great potential in her even if she's not able to see it currently. Obedience is her answer; she's listening to God and exercising discipline. I'm confident that her daily deposits of purpose will be rewarded. There's a grand prize after the race if we push through, yield to wise counsel, and fight off our yearning for instant gratification.

Choosing the Right Door

The moment you are getting close to fully operating in your purpose, you will be presented with derailing options. Choices of things that may feel like new opportunities but are merely options to prolong what you ultimately want to achieve. Stay the course by focusing on making daily deposits towards your purpose, not your pleasure. That's the CHEAT CODE!

I've been asked this online many times. How do you discern which door to open? The one that connects to your purpose. That's why it's so important to be confident that you know your purpose.

For example, I will use my personal journey as a musician. Once upon a time I pursued music heavily with a few of my friends Thomas, Phillip, and Jerrold. We formed a group that created a marginal community buzz in our own right. Our album received stellar reviews and was overall a good body of work.

After the release of that project, I started writing a book of poems and decided to stop rapping. Within the same week, I was contacted with two totally separate opportunities. One was to be featured on a song that I'm embarrassed to say the title of and, secondly, to perform a poem live I had posted online at a club in Atlanta called Apache. I did both but my flesh enjoyed recording more. I found more pleasure in partying in the studio and showing a braggadocious side of myself. If I was faced with the two options today, I would only go with the one attached to my purpose.

One of my purposes is to be an author. My entire life I have been told I was great at writing. I was using my gift of writing as something I enjoyed doing but it didn't honor God because of the content.

The road to purpose gets rough in our microwave society. Information is out there for anyone to start a business or career in anything instantly. We must withhold from the simple pleasure of titles and instant gratification. This process may feel like a punishment at times but it's your development. The process is gradual and requires faith in God's timeline.

One of the biggest wastes of time for men is chasing women. The biggest waste of time for women is chasing love. Both highly inefficient. The door you should be investing your time in is your purpose. Every day is a war between pleasure and purpose. What I desire to do in the moment and what I desire to do the most. The nature you feed determines your future.

The new Brian D. Williams cost me the old one. To become the version of myself God required, I could no longer do all of the things I used to do. I had to hold myself to a higher standard of living. You deserve the best, but you must be ok shedding your past. This includes shedding old habits.

There was a time that my checking Facebook was muscle memory. Anytime I sat down, I would pull my phone out of my pocket, moving my thumbs super-fast, selecting the Facebook app. I didn't even have to think about it. Now, I wake up with a different muscle memory. What's the one deposit I can do today that I will thank myself for later? Ask yourself this every day, and you will spend more time investing in you than entertaining yourself.

Keep putting the work in and write down a few pleasures that you indulge in. Use this list to focus on cutting them out of your daily activity for good. Fast from harmful pleasures and find an accountability partner you don't mind being completely transparent with.

There's nothing wrong with having a good time. Keep in mind, daily entertainment is not necessary for the road you are traveling. Pleasure should be used in moments of recharge instead of the reverse. Some use pleasure as a mandatory activity to make them feel they are really living life. Don't get tricked into thinking all life's fulfillment comes only from the moments you had fun in. In the end, the things you did to help others will be remembered, not what you've done for your own pleasures.

You should be able to analyze the type of day you had on a daily basis. Ask yourself, did I make a deposit that my future self will be able to spend or did I spend today's time in enjoyment and entertainment? Maybe today was a perfect balance between the two. You have a greater likelihood towards success on your terms when purpose and pleasure are balanced in your life.

CHAPTER 6

○ ○ ○

Purpose Comparison

Not that we dare to classify or compare ourselves with some of those who are commending themselves. But when they measure themselves by one another and compare themselves with one another, they are without understanding.

2 Corinthians 10:12

The first time I heard the quote, "Comparison is the thief of joy," was from one of my favorite rappers although I know he did not originate the saying. Joy is a moving target. Once you think you've hit the target, it moves another 100 yards further. It will leave you in the state of never being satisfied and always looking for the next goal to achieve. Most people would like to have something that they don't have to do the work to obtain. It's easy to compare your life to someone who you believe has your version of success. In the midst of you comparing, more than likely, you are remaining still. This chapter covers ways to prevent being stagnant and operating in your purpose.

It's extremely difficult to create the momentum necessary for you to create impactful things for the world if you are constantly monitoring and comparing your life to someone else's. Comparing can cause jealousy and envy. A study released in 2020 argued that 12% of our daily thought is spent on some form of comparison. God makes no mistakes. If he wanted you to be like someone else, He would have made you like someone else. To make the most out of what He has given to only you, accept that you are different and capitalize off your uniqueness. Completing the steps in the discovery process allows you to not have a need to compare yourself with anyone.

A sound heart is life to the body, but envy is rottenness to the bones.

Proverbs 14:30 (NKJV)

We all have our own gifts; yet sometimes we would prefer someone else's.

Growing up, I had a friend named Nick who was extremely athletic. He could run faster and jump higher than anyone in the school. He lived across the street from me, and he would come over often to play basketball in my backyard. I often got the best of him because I practiced shooting and dribbling more often than he did. I developed skills that he had yet to acquire up to that point. Basketball was fun to me, so I played daily at my convenience. With the basketball court being in my backyard, I organized tournaments, created drills, and played everyone in bordering neighborhoods to test my skill level.

Nick moved away and, for years, I lost contact with him. These were the years before social media. So when someone moved, there was a possibility you would never see that person again. Years later, at the age of 15 while walking down my high school hallway, I ran into Nick. He'd just transferred to my school as a new student. He was at least 6'2" and wanted nothing more than to challenge me again at basketball. Ironically, I lived at the same house with the same court.

What Nick failed to mention at the time was he'd signed up for recreational basketball over the previous few years. At this rec center, his basketball IQ grew to another level. Needless to say, Nick came back and punished me to a score that, 20 years later, I will still never reveal. I can outwork someone who has put no effort in developing their gift, but I could never outwork Nick's natural athleticism, height, speed, and wingspan once he learned skill. At that point I wished I had those gifts. It robbed me of the joy that I had for the game of basketball. At a young age, I couldn't understand why I no longer reigned supreme on my court. I could have continued to focus on being a natural leader on the court and honed my skills, but I constantly compared the benefits of having his gifts.

Instead of desiring another gift, guess what? There's something you can do that someone can never mimic. Monetize your gift for the kingdom of God. What I didn't recognize at the time was Nick's success in basketball didn't equal my failure. Just because he's great doesn't mean I'm inadequate. This recognition was one of the many things that helped me on my journey of self-discovery. It allowed me to continue to search for what I was better at than most and what came natural to me. If I noticed something I did in life that was easy for me but challenging for others, I would encourage them, not compare or tear them down.

Another example comes from my favorite 90's sitcom "Martin." There's an episode where the main character, Martin, is preparing to attend his class reunion. He wants to win the "the man of the decade" award at his high school class reunion which signifies he was the most successful person in the class. He asked his girlfriend to go to the beauty salon, spa, and dentist to prepare for a night of proving why he should be the recipient of this award. His girlfriend, Gina, obliged. While she was at the dentist, they accidentally hit a nerve in her mouth, and she was over-drugged with pain medication. She also received an avocado face mask which she was allergic to.

Needless to say, Gina wasn't looking her best for Martin's "big day." Embarrassed with Gina's current condition, he asked her to stay home and skip the class reunion event. He later learned that his constant comparison to his classmates was unnecessary. After interacting with everyone, he realized that their opinions didn't matter as much as he initially thought. He was trying to impress people who didn't truly care about him.

Is there something you are holding off giving to the world because you are comparing it to what someone else would do? Be careful not to let the chaos of comparison into your daily life.

Social Media Flu
The world is rapidly changing from the influences of

social media. We are able to create elaborate personas and exaggerate events for exposure from the convenience of our phones. This has increased the amount of purpose comparison. Too much social media can put your confidence in the dumps. What we see daily affects our mental health and can even subconsciously impact our self-esteem. Popular social media apps like Facebook, Twitter, Instagram, and TikTok allow individuals the opportunity to create highlight reels of the best moments of their lives.

Always remember...no one is posting their failures. If we are not careful, if we view something from someone else's account that we aspire to do, we can begin to compare.

There are four ways to avoid the social media flu.

Appreciate what you currently possess.
Remind yourself that some of the things you prayed for years prior, you currently have. I was definitely guilty at different points of my life of not appreciating my blessings. My health, my family, my home, a reliable car are just a few things I prayed for and received. I recall being at the dealership praying that the car I liked would be in my price range after they ran my credit. I drove off the lot with the car I desired. Just one year later, I found myself wanting something more luxurious. From that day

forward, I committed to practicing gratitude. Regularly reminding myself to be thankful for the things I have and to stop focusing on the next big thing to chase.

Remind yourself that social media is not real.
The posts on social media are designed to get your attention. These posts are formulated. Many of the things and items captured in the picture, reel, or video are not real. Posts are designed to get you to like, follow, or comment on the post. Every time you look at these manufactured photos for hours day in and day out, you begin to believe that their lives are superior to yours. Depositing hours of luxurious activities in your subconscious can lead you to make horrible decisions in an attempt to compete with others. If you are single, looking at couples' Instagram can maybe allow you to entertain someone who is not compatible with you because you desire the companionship of the couple you are following. Or purchasing a car or home that you can't afford because you saw your cousin posting his new home on Facebook. Maintain a healthy diet of what you allow yourself to see and hear.

Recently it was reported that a celebrity DJ committed suicide. The day before, he posted a video on social media smiling, dancing, and projecting nothing but happiness. This is one of the many examples of influencers posting what they want you to see but not how they feel in reality. He was able to mask his true feelings for a 15-to-30 second TikTok. Protect yourself with the armor of God and evade the pitfalls of depressing thoughts.

Be selective in who you follow.
Everything you allow yourself to see, hear, or be within your personal space affects you. This applies to social media as well. If you follow an account or page on social media and it triggers negative emotions...unfollow the page. Trust your instincts and keep good mental health practices by choosing to keep leveled emotions. Some pages may be suggested by social media for you to follow based on algorithms that don't apply to you. View the page to get a sample of the content presented and make a decision on whether their content serves a purpose in your life. Does the content on the page give you joy? Assist in fulfilling your purpose? Help you become a better person?

In generations before us, they had a similar decision to make but it was choosing the best newspaper publication to read. Choose your information source wisely. They may be able to push a narrative if you are triggered instantly to compare your life to the content of a content creator's. Something could be wrong with the page, not you. Some pages are designed to make people jealous and envious. Don't relinquish your power. Be selective about who you follow regardless of the their follow count and engagement.

Social Media Break

Since we already know how social media can be bad, we should find ways to limit our access. Recent studies show that limiting the use of social media to 30 minutes a day significantly reduced feelings of depression and loneliness. After using it for a time, the algorithm can be so great that it will only recommend pages and posts you are interested in. This causes you to continue using the app or website much longer than anticipated. It's often referred to as the rabbit hole. You initially tend to only use social media for a moment but when distracted, one moment can turn into an hour.

I recommend taking a break from social media at least one day a week and limiting the use of it to less than an hour a day and no more than 30 minutes each use. Placing a restriction on this can help to not get wrapped up in something that is not beneficial to you. For example, there will always be a new celebrity gossip story. You can spend a lot of time being unproductive, arguing your opinions in the comment section under a post. How does that serve you in making you a better person and operating in your purpose? We can become whatever we would like on social media including a judge, but is that the correct way to use the platform? It's best to use it in a way to amplify your purpose and display your gift.

Scrolling mindlessly on social media only places you as the consumer to be subjected to whatever it wants to sell you that day. Decide on a length of time that works best for your schedule (under an hour) and be productive. Break away from it at least one day a week and one month a year. You can let your close friends and family know you are taking a break; especially, if you are an active poster just so they don't worry when you become inactive.

Delete the app from your phone, many people check social media reflexively. At the height of my own social media addiction, I would unlock my phone and instantly go to Twitter without thinking about it.

Connecting to your purpose can be a difference maker. Figure out how you can spend more time with God and be productive by removing yourself from wasteful activities. Replace the time you spend on social media with a hobby, task, or activity to change your trajectory.

Don't be envious of someone else's journey. A story I always enjoy in the spirit of comparison is the elephant and the dog. An elephant and a dog become pregnant at the same time. Three months down the line, the dog gave birth to six puppies and 6 months later the dog was pregnant again. At 9 months it gave birth to six puppies. At 18 months, the dog approached the elephant and asked, "Are you sure you are pregnant? We became pregnant on the same date, and you have yet to give birth to your baby. What is taking your baby so long?"

The elephant replied, "There's something I want you to

understand. What I am carrying is not a puppy. My pregnancy takes 2 years, and when my baby hits the ground, the earth feels it. When my baby crosses the road people stop to watch in admiration."

Don't lose faith when you see others receive answers to their prayers in what seems like record time. Don't be discouraged, understand your time is coming. When it hits the surface of the earth, people shall yield in admiration.

Strategies to Break Free From Purpose Comparison

Reconnecting with Your Values

The best way to combat purpose comparison is to reconnect with what matters most to you. Values are the guiding principles that give meaning to our lives and influence our decisions. When you focus on your own values, you become less concerned with how others are living their lives. In the first chapter, we discussed taking an inventory and identifying your core values. Use these values as a source to constantly connect with.

Embrace Your Unique Path

Your journey is yours alone. A journey that no one can duplicate exactly. The experiences, challenges, and skills that have shaped you are different from anyone else's.

Embracing this uniqueness allows you to focus on the progress you're making rather than the distance between you and others. Similar to a track meet, you will only get so far running a race and constantly looking behind you. This slows your momentum. Embracing who you are with no shame and accepting your gifts will allow you to break free from comparison.

Celebrate Your Wins

No matter how small, each step forward is a victory. I will get a victory meal for any goal I can cross off my list. Any of my friends can attest to this. When I get new clients, I treat myself to a steak dinner. Create a habit of celebrating your accomplishments, even if they don't seem as impressive as others' achievements. Keep records of the goals you've accomplished to remind yourself of the wins you've gotten over the years.

Shift from Competition to Inspiration

Instead of feeling envious when you see someone living out their purpose, try to view their journey as inspiration. Ask yourself, "What can I learn from their path?" or "How can their story encourage me in my own journey?" Taking this positive spin can allow you to properly motivate yourself towards success instead of comparing. Reading a book about someone's successes in a field of interest for you can help change your trajectory instantly.

Purpose comparison can be an insidiously unproductive

habit. It prevents you from understanding the unique value of your own path, leading to feelings of inadequacy and self-doubt. By reconnecting with your values, celebrating uniqueness, and practicing gratitude, you can return the focus back to what really matters - finding your purpose! Remember, your journey is not a race against others; rather it should be seen as an exploration of what makes life meaningful to you. By foregoing comparison and living without limits or expectations, comparison frees us all up to create lives that are purposeful yet authentically ours.

Philippians 2:3 says, "Don't be selfish; don't try to impress others. Be humble, thinking of others as better than yourselves."

CHAPTER 7

○ ○ ○

Change Trajectory

So my dear brothers and sisters, be strong and immovable. Always work enthusiastically for the Lord, for you know that nothing you do for the Lord is ever useless.

1 Corinthians 15:58

Your behavior, daily habits, thoughts, and the people you surround yourself with will determine your trajectory. Pastor Dale Bronner once said, "Discipline is about valuing what you want most over what you want now! Discipline involves delaying personal gratification." The most important word in that quote is "value." What you value is the fuel that keeps you moving towards what you want to accomplish in life. We discussed in the previous chapters the pitfalls of losing your purpose, pleasure or purpose, Satan's tricks, or purpose comparison. It's imperative that you do the work to avoid these things. Your daily habits are what will change your trajectory to the land of prosperity.

Daily Habits

An important question to ask yourself would be, "Am I heading in the right direction based upon what I do daily?" I was once asked in college, the prestigious and unsinkable Albany State University, to view my life as if my purpose was a missile. The intended target is to live a life of purpose. To hit your target, you have to adjust the trajectory of the missile daily. Many people don't view the success of navigating in your passion as a compilation of many adjustments. They see it as only a few adjustments and that's incorrect. It's consistently making the right decisions and adjusting your life to change your trajectory. If you were out of time and no more adjustments were made to the direction of your missile, where would it land?

The current state of my new business venture would crash and burn if I could no longer make adjustments. At its current state, I could not give this business to my children.

We change our trajectory by making a daily decision to complete something that brings us closer to our goal. Have you ever spent an entire day doing nothing? While there's nothing wrong with that, too many nothing days will put us in a position of doing the opposite of what we want to achieve. A pastor I often watch, Michael Todd, said in a sermon recently, "Every day you choose to fill up two cups: your flesh cup or your purpose cup." Even when I do nothing, I'm giving in to my flesh to watch bad TV programs or have one too many drinks. This is ultimately not contributing to my purpose. While educating myself through an audio book would be an example of filling my purpose cup.

Once you recognize how you can improve your daily habits, it is best to fast away from your flesh desires. I had an unhealthy relationship with social media as I discussed in the previous chapters. After deleting the social media apps on my phone for 21 days, I was able to break the habit of time I would spend on them. Changing my trajectory means I'm decisively making a step a day to create the momentum needed to hit my destination. Sowing seeds in 2025 can reap a harvest for 2026. To do so, you would have to be active in the present.

Pursuing Your Purpose

Stepping into your purpose can be an incredible achievement, but its real transformation comes when integrated into daily practice. Your purpose shouldn't just be an aspirational concept, it should guide every aspect of your life! This chapter will show how aligning routines, habits, and decisions with your purpose can give a greater sense of fulfillment every day.

Living life with purpose does not involve making significant, immediate changes. It's about taking small, deliberate steps that align with your values and purpose statement. These might include choosing activities that matter more to you or being mindful of how others treat you. Over time these tiny adjustments can create a life that better reflects what's truly desired of you.

Align Your Daily Activities

Achieving a meaningful life means being aware of how you spend your time. Many individuals feel misaligned with their purpose due to spending too much time doing activities that do not matter; such as time-consuming tasks, obligations no longer fitting your values, or distractions that pull their attention away from what matters to them.

Are You Spending Too Much Time Sitting Around Doing Nothing?

Take an honest assessment of how you currently spend your time. Which activities bring you closer to fulfilling your purpose? Which activities hinder it? By prioritizing what really matters in life, you'll create space for it all to blossom.

I enjoy completing an exercise once a week that shows me where I am clearer than a bank balance. If you open your banking app, it's going to show you how much money is in your account. Similarly, if you complete this exercise weekly you will know where you stand in your purpose journey. This exercise consists of writing down what I do each day and how much time I devote to each activity. At the end of the week, I categorize each activity into three groups.

Align With My Purpose

There are three categories of activities to consider when evaluating how you spend your time. First, purpose-aligned activities are those that resonate with your core values and strengths, bringing you joy and fulfillment. These activities support your overall sense of purpose and align with who you are. Next, neutral activities are the essential tasks, such as chores or errands, that neither directly support nor conflict with your purpose but are necessary to maintain daily life. Finally, there are misaligned activities, which are tasks that feel draining or unfulfilling, pulling your energy away from what truly matters and hinder your progress toward your goals. Recognizing these distinctions can help you prioritize your time more effectively.

Consider how you might decrease the time you devote to activities from the second category while increasing the time you invest in those from the first one. Habits are the cornerstones of daily life. They set your routine and, ultimately, your direction in life. Purposeful habits are those that align with your values and bring you closer to realizing your purpose. For example, if helping others is part of your mission statement, then making time to check-in with a friend might become part of your routine each day. While many neutral activities are necessary, if you spend a lot of time running errands you may want to find another way to optimize your time. And, of course, tasks that do not align with my purpose should remain at a minimum. Building new habits takes time and consistency. Begin with one small habit that aligns with your purpose, and work on incorporating it into your routine until it becomes second nature.

Determine which aspect of your purpose you would like to focus on each day of your daily life, and then create a simple habit aligning with this focus. For example, if creativity is part of your purpose, then spend 10 minutes each day journaling or drawing as part of this habit. Use a habit tracker or reminders to help ensure you remain consistent for at least 30 days. Smart phone reminder apps have helped aid many professionals better manage their tasks.

Purposeful Decision-Making

Living life with purpose includes making daily decisions that reflect your values. When faced with a decision, ask yourself whether it fits with the life you wish to create–this could range from choosing how to spend free time, or more complex issues like making career changes.

Purposeful decision-making helps you stay true to what matters most in life, even during difficult moments. This means saying "yes" only to opportunities that align with your purpose while remaining open-minded enough to reject those that don't. By integrating purpose into your daily decisions and habits, you will see how small changes can lead to an enriching life.

Time to Develop

Changing your trajectory won't happen overnight. It takes study, friendships, and a relationship with God. Get out of the place where ambition dies, the LAND OF COM-FORT. For me, networking was not something I was passionate about. I believe it was a hit on my ego that I needed an outer source to be successful. Also, networking was a personality conflict because I wasn't a social butterfly. It took me longer to develop meaningful relationships. I had to study who was a part of an organization or chamber of commerce before I attended meetings/gatherings along with their interests so I could talk to them with confidence. I attended monthly events regularly and created friendships. In time, people began to associate me with the cleaning business and would give me whatever leads they came across.

Throughout this process my relationships with God and the Holy Spirit were paramount. It allowed me not to rush the process or look at every new relationship, new colleague, or business owner I was introduced to as a dollar sign. Trusting in what God has for me and no one else. We are not created as a carbon copy but one of a kind. Sometimes we think we are ready for an opportunity only to later find out that we may be lacking something needed to elevate to the next level. I fully trust the process I'm currently in. Going to the gym for 9 hours won't give you the results you are looking for. However, going to the gym 1 hour a day for 9 days straight is a good start.

It's often glossed over that in the Bible, David was developed not discovered. It took many years for him to become King of Israel. He was intentionally put through a very rigorous training regime. No other king documented went through the trials David went through which is why no one was as successful as him.

One example was shown in 2 Samuel 16. King David arrived in Bahurim and was approached by Shimei from the house of Saul. Shimei was upset that David was now the king God favored. He began to curse and throw things while falsely accusing David of things that were not true. David's king guard was puzzled that David did not give the order for him to be killed. The reason David ignored the insults was because of the training he went through for this moment. Even after he was questioned by one of the guards, David remained unbothered because of what he learned early in development. David learned that God's will is more important than his ego. There was nothing that could be said or done to remove him from the purpose over his life.

After you finish your development, you will have confidence in the direction you are heading in through God. It being shown to him in a myriad of ways prior that God's will is paramount. To change your trajectory, you have to be unwavering and determined.

There is no firm knowledge of what happened in Jesus' life from the age of 17-33. It is heavily assumed He was going through a period of development. Even though He knew exactly what His purpose was, it was still necessary for the king of kings to be developed. David was given the promise that one day he would be king at the age of 17; yet, he didn't sit on the throne until the age of 30. Allow time for God to develop your character for the dreams you request.

Nothing I enjoy eating is prepared quickly. There's a

difference between microwaved meals and dinners prepared at Ruth's Chris. I pray to remain patient while I prepare myself for opportunities that God puts before me. I believe in God's timing to develop me for my purpose.

Levels to This

God will test you with the minimum before you are trusted to manage the maximum. The more tests you pass and manage what you currently have access to, the more access you'll get to the next level. The tests are given not to deny or delay you on the road to your purpose. The tests are given to develop you. The problems you continue to face let you know God wants to position you for something greater. Once you figure out the problem, an invitation is given to you to get in front of your purpose.

I believe so many parallels were intentionally put all around us to help us understand the process, sometimes we just choose to ignore them. Grade school, farming, and sports are just a few examples of parallels with levels that must be mastered before participants are presented with new opportunities. To become a professional football player, you must statistically impress a high school head coach, a college coach, and an NFL scout or general manager. While it is possible to skip one, there are still levels you must pass. You could be an average athlete in high school and change your trajectory by adjusting your daily habits, but it's still a level you must surpass. There are levels to everything we do, and we must commit to the process for our purpose to manifest. Try to journal your goal and break it down into actionable steps. As you achieve your goals, continue to add steps until you reach your version of success. Here's a sample chart below:

High School Football Team Goal to start at wide receiver by the end of football camp:

Increase my 40-speed time: Change my workout frequency from 3 days a week to 5 days a week

Improve catching skills: Do catching drills 7 days a week

Learning new route running techniques: Sign up for 3-day receiver skill camp

Better my endurance: Go on a Keto diet

Changing Your Perspective

Changing the way you look at life tasks and challenges will change your trajectory. Romans 12:2 states, "Do not be conformed to this world, but be transformed by the renewal of your mind, that by testing you may discern what is the will of God, what is good and acceptable and perfect." Renew your mind by spending time daily studying the bible. Also, read or listen to audiobooks in your purpose field to continue your education. The more you know the more you grow, and it can change the way you ultimately see life. Instead of saying, "I got to do…" try saying, "I get to do."

I would sometimes be guilty of praying for the opportunity to become a business owner, then years later complain about how heavy the workload is. Well, I prayed for it. Lol. Understand that looking at things from the perspective of the cup being half-full instead of half-empty can help you continue to push forward. Thinking negative thoughts, complaining, or constantly feeling the need to vent about your work day is not necessary. Each day you have the opportunity to pursue and be active in your purpose is a blessing. Two people can see the same thing but describe it in two different ways. You have to be intentional about being positive and trusting the process of your development. Looking at life from a negative perspective will slow your process and you may begin to procrastinate. While looking at your current place in a positive light, you will continue to work towards being greater in your purpose.

Hurdles

Jump the first hurdle before thinking about jumping all 10. This thought process is simple, but many people are confused by it. It means instead of thinking about the task in its entirety and how overwhelming it can be, think about what you need to do to get the project started. If you are racing the 100-meter hurdles, most track athletes gain the most confidence to compete after successfully jumping the first hurdle. The first hurdle is "I'm not good enough...I'm too young...I'm not smart enough...I come from a single parent household." It should be muscle memory or reflex for you to denounce any of these thoughts because they prevent you from clearing the hurdle and building the momentum necessary for you to reach your true potential. Jump the first hurdle but don't celebrate just yet, there's another hurdle in 10 meters.

Catch You Up

There's a wonderful parable in Matthew that I recently pulled something new from relating to changing our trajectory. After Jesus finished feeding 5,000 people, he went up to the mountain to pray in isolation. He intentionally asked the disciples to leave without Him on the boat and start the journey. When Jesus finished praying, he was aware that the boat would be a considerable distance away from Him. He didn't ask the disciples to wait until he was done spending time with God on the mountain.

Jesus caught up to the boat by walking on water. This is one of the many examples that shows God will catch you up to your rightful position. He will never let us fall behind if we are giving our time to Him. Trust in His plan and He will put you back on track. Allow him to develop you and provide growth in the areas that will prepare you for your next season. "Seek first his kingdom and his righteousness and all things will be given to you as well" Matthew 6:33.

In my attempt to restate the theme of this chapter, it can be summarized by the subchapters. You can change your trajectory by watching your daily habits, allowing time for development, understanding there are levels to change, and changing your perspective. Since at some point none of us know our purpose, once we realize what it is, we must change our trajectory in the direction of our purpose. It will take time to develop a sense of what to do and how to govern yourself in different situations with this newfound knowledge. Stay the course and make minor adjustments to get a major impact in your life. And remind yourself that even in the process of starting over, God will catch you up.

CHAPTER 8

Purpose Confirmed

And they went forth, and preached everywhere, the Lord working with them, and confirming the word with signs following. Amen.

Mark 16:20

There may be no greater feeling than using the talents and gifts God blessed you with and feeling the confirmation that you are in the right place. It's literally one of life's greatest mysteries. We all came to Earth with a gift, and to unwrap that gift in its full potential is an amazing feeling. It's the one thing that no one can figure out for you, you must travel on this journey of purpose confirmation alone. To confirm means to establish the truth. Purpose confirmation is determining the truth about the will over your life. To further the kingdom's agenda, more Christians finding their purpose from the circus allows us to spread the gospel, so more people are saved.

When you know your purpose, you have a clear understanding of what you want to achieve or what you want to do with your life. Having a sense of purpose can give direction and meaning to your actions and decisions, leading to a more fulfilling life. It can also provide motivation and drive, making it easier to work towards your goals and overcome challenges along the way. However, finding one's purpose can be a lifelong journey and may involve isolated self-reflection, discovery, and experimentation. You will feel a certain level of peace and serenity. This chapter's purpose is to explain the signs to confirm you have arrived!

Everything is Suddenly a Coincidence

Now that you are intentionally attempting to operate in

your purpose and fulfill it, opportunities will arise. They will come to you in the form of coincidences, but this is from a God who knows the amount of hairs on your head (Luke 12:7). It means you are operating in His favor and grace. Coincidences refers to the occurrence of two or more events at the same time or place in a manner that appears to be more than just a mere chance. It's when two or more things happen at the same time in a way that seem to be connected or related, but may not actually be related causally. Things will align in a way that seem to be orchestrated. It's your season, it's your time, and you are in the right place.

An example of a coincidence on your journey to purpose may be meeting an influencer or a potential mentor you know personally but had no idea you shared interests with. Or meeting a family member at a family reunion who can give you an opportunity without the drawn out process. God brings blessings into our lives through people around us. The coincidence is God's favor and approval of our current path. Relationships will make more sense. Also, you will be able to further confirm without question why certain people are in your life.

Operating with this new form of clarity you can see exactly why someone is detrimental to your purpose. Simply because you know your purpose. Sometimes it's not even intentional, they just are not good for you at the moment. It's not your responsibility to understand why, just have faith in the God who knows all. You will be able to operate with clarity you have never seen before. Satan is the author of confusion but now since you have confirmed your purpose, you will begin to experience the opposite of that which is certainty. Moving with certainty is the way to the destination. The coincidence is your steps being ordered by God.

You Feel Inspired to Change Something

Another way your purpose is confirmed is through inspiration to change something and provide a solution to a problem. We are problem solvers by nature. Nothing fuels us to completion more than an easy fix. How many times have you taken over a task that wasn't being done correctly? My mom would often take over for me in the kitchen when she saw I wasn't making the dinner correctly. Between me and you, I would purposely do things incorrectly so she would step in.

Working to aid or fix a problem that aligns with your core values gives a level of fulfillment unachievable through any other action. Changing the world starts with small steps and making a positive impact in your community. You can get involved in some local volunteer work, advocacy, or start a project that addresses a specific issue you're passionate about. Remember to set achievable goals, stay focused, and stay determined. Every little bit helps, and collectively, small actions can lead to big change.

The problem you have an answer for will seem so obvious to you but not to others. Your unique life experiences and education have prepared you for this moment to fill a void. The moment to uniquely resolve an issue or add something to the world to make it a better place. You were strategically put in a place to be exposed to a problem that only you could be inspired to change. Many people experience loss in a certain area of society and dedicate their lives to fixing the problem. A colleague lost his mother to cancer, then subsequently started a non-profit to aid women with breast cancer and raise money for cure research. We are all inspired by different causes. That cause can push you to become active enough to confirm your purpose.

Money is No Longer the Motivation

Many have pursued a 9-to-5 career that paid the highest salary and offered the best benefit package. When your purpose is confirmed, money is no longer the sole motivation. Being compensated is secondary to taking action that fulfills, is easy to complete, and challenges you. You will be able to operate at an extremely high level and people will pay you well for that. Simply compare yourself being highly motivated and having a God-given talent to someone doing the same thing just for money. You will not only go above and beyond the standard service level, but you will also be very knowledgeable in a particular field of interest. It's a well-known fact that there are many people working every day in a field they dislike but it pays them well. It's possible to obtain wealth outside the kingdom of God but it comes with unhappiness. Sacrificing a life to be financially stable but is void of joy is not a life anyone wants to live intentionally. As discussed in previous chapters, the obsession is a very unfulfilling and insatiable trip. Once you arrive in purpose, confirmed money will be a bonus to the fulfillment.

Your Past Makes Sense

Many of the trials and tribulations life presents us have a greater purpose. Even when we do things we are not supposed to do, they can be used for a greater purpose through the will of God. Abraham lied, Moses was a murderer, David committed adultery, Peter had a bad temper, Noah was an alcoholic, Paul was a murderer and God still used all of them.

Paul had one of the best metaphors in the bible in 2 Corinthians 12:7. "Even though I have received such wonderful revelations from God. So to keep me from becoming proud, I was given a thorn in my flesh, a messenger from Satan to torment me and keep me from becoming proud." This verse is only one of the many examples of God using something from the past to humble us but still keep us chucking along to change our trajectory. The thorn was an uncomfortable reminder of what happened in the past but not significant enough to halt Paul's progress in Christ.

Your past can fall short of His glory but you have to get up and continue. Jesus is advocating for you at the side of God and God's mercies are new every morning. You are the righteousness of God and now have the opportunity to maximize your potential. God will use your blemished past. When reflecting on your life to the current day and time, suddenly the incident that happened many years ago in your life connects to the reason you are here. You are now able to realize why certain trials, tribulations, and even people were present in your life. If your purpose is to become a nurse in a hospital and when you were in high school, you immediately acted to aid someone who injured themselves, receiving praise from staff or school administration may be the validation needed for you to attend nursing school.

I enjoy taking time to myself to appreciate the obstacles now because they truly made me who I am today. Without my past experiences, I would be ill-equipped to handle and properly utilize my gifts and talents towards my purpose. I am thankful that while I didn't appreciate some of the toughest moments in my life that were probably the result of bad decision making, I needed them for growth and maturity. Now I'm comforted by the fact that if I keep him first, I can live a joyous life. God can turn anything that was meant for bad for my good and confirm my purpose process.

Flow State

Your purpose has been confirmed, and you are now operating with full confidence in the kingdom of God. One of my favorite movies growing up was, "The Last Dragon." This movie was about a young boy named Bruce Leroy who was searching for the master so he could reach the ultimate level of martial arts mastery referred to as, "The Glow." He was challenged in every aspect of his life. His family was attacked, his romantic interest was kidnapped, and he lacked confidence in his martial arts abilities. After being pushed to his breaking point, he realized the master he was seeking was within. He then achieved his final form with no effort.

Many of us have not spent the time with just ourselves to figure what greatness we are capable of. When you're pursuing your purpose, you often experience a state of flow (which could be referred to as "The Glow"), where you're fully immersed in what you're doing and lose track of time. This indicates a sense of alignment and engagement with your chosen path. You no longer have to force anything because everything comes with no effort. It's simple, second nature, a part of you, and so easy that you lose track of time. You are able to complete things with ease that look very difficult to others. All of the time investments you have made studying or working on your craft now fit perfectly like pieces of a puzzle. A purpose statement can help assist you in getting your GLOW!

A purpose statement is a clear, succinct declaration of

your goals and ambitions. It should capture what motivates and drives you and what contributions you want to make to society; unlike mission statements which focus on doing something specific, purpose statements consider deeper reasons behind why one does what they're doing. It took me some time to develop my purpose statement, but once it came, it provided so much clarity. I wrote my first purpose statement with an Expo marker on my bathroom mirror. It was a daily reminder of the seed of purpose I needed to nourish and protect from distraction.

Purpose statements should reflect who you are right now and the things that are most important to you, with the goal of becoming something tangible you can refer back to when making decisions or facing challenges. They're never fixed in stone–instead, they can evolve over time as your life and priorities shift. Your purpose statement should feel authentic and inspirational so it can act as a guide when facing decisions or challenging moments in life.

Crafting Your Statement

When formulating your purpose statement, take into account these essential components:

Your Values:
What principles guide your actions and decisions?

Your Passions:
Which activities, causes, or subjects make you come alive?

Your Strengths:
Which skills or qualities come naturally to you?

Your Experiences: Have there been any moments or challenges which have altered the course of your life that have helped to shape who you are?

Drafting this statement solidifies and confirms your purpose. It can be a short sentence that expresses all your values, passions, and strengths along with how you hope to make a difference in the world. For example: "My purpose is to act by employing my strengths for [outcome or impact]."

Refine your purpose statement until it feels right for you; it doesn't need to be perfect, just something that resonates. Make your purpose statement visible--write it on a sticky note or journal--so you can refer back to it regularly. Here are examples of purpose statements I received from my men's group.

"My mission is to spark creativity in others through storytelling and art."

"My aim is to foster an environment in which everyone feels seen and heard by advocating for mental health awareness."

"My objective is to foster children's love of learning by being an encouraging educator."

Once You Have Drafted Your Purpose Statement
Now that you have written your draft purpose statement, use it as a decision-making tool when facing choices or challenges in life. When facing choices or dilemmas, ask yourself whether these align with my purpose statement and support its deeper meaning in my life? A strong purpose statement should act as a compass, providing guidance in times of confusion or doubt. It should reflect who you are as an individual even if it remains incomplete at this point in time. I will share my purpose statement as an example:

My purpose as an author is to inspire and empower readers through stories and insights that encourage self-discovery, resilience, and the pursuit of a meaningful life. I strive to create a connection with my audience, offering them guidance, comfort, and a new perspective through my words. By sharing my experiences and the lessons I've learned, I aim to help others navigate their own journeys and discover their unique purpose, fostering a sense of hope and possibility in each reader's life.

Crafting your purpose statement is a significant milestone on your journey. It takes all of the self-reflection and exploration you've done and distills it into a clear sense of direction. In the next chapter, we'll explore how to integrate your purpose into your daily life and arrive empty.

"His lord said unto him, Well done, thou good and faithful servant thou hast been faithful over a few things, I will make thee ruler over many things."

Matthew 25:21

N othing I create will ever be perfect. I can only release it and give it the opportunity to be improved. Even this book had its challenges of me holding on to it too long because I wanted my first book to be a New York Times Bestseller. The title of this chapter simply means to be intentional every day. Life can easily be determined by the sum of your actions while on Earth. Life is designed for you to live abundantly by operating in your purpose.

Deuteronomy 31:8 says "The Lord himself will go before you and will be with you; he will never leave you nor forsake you." God will go before you, but He won't go for you. Fulfilling your potential while here will ensure you arrive in heaven with purpose fulfilled. The phrase "arrive to heaven empty" typically refers to the idea that when we die, we will not bring any material possessions or accomplishments with us to the afterlife. Instead, it suggests the only thing that matters after leaving this Earth is the spiritual state of the individual. We are all created with a purpose which has been established in the earlier chapters of this book. This phrase is often used to encourage people to focus on their character, their relationships, and their spiritual growth while they are alive, rather than obsessing over material possessions or accomplishments that will ultimately be left behind. Unlock your potential while you have the opportunity to do so.

I hope you have your number two pencil ready because it's testing time! How can you be faithful with "the few" to increase your management to "the many?" My favorite parable in the bible is the theme scripture for this chapter, Matthew 25:21. In this parable, a man going on a journey entrusts his property to his servants. To one he gives five talents, to another he gives two talents, and a third person receives one talent, each according to his ability.

The servant with five talents invests them and earns five more. The servant with two talents does the same and earns two more. However, the servant with one talent buries it in the ground. When the master returns, he praises the first two servants for their diligence and rewards them with greater responsibilities. The master rebukes the third servant for his laziness and fear, taking away the one talent and giving it to the servant with ten talents. The unfaithful servant is cast into the outer darkness.

The highlight of this parable shows the importance of using the gifts and resources God has given us. It teaches that faithfulness and diligence in using our talents for God's purposes will be rewarded, while neglect and fear will lead to loss and punishment. It emphasizes accountability and the expectation that believers actively engage in God's work. How can you double your talents and arrive with the job completed? By not living in fear and focusing on what God has put on the inside of you.

Another important part of this parable is how many

talents were given. There is no coincidence that the servant who received just one talent got the fewest and did absolutely nothing with it. The servants being faithful to what was placed in their hands and managing it well provided an increase. God places you as steward of a one-of-a-kind purpose potential seed inside of you. Manage it well and you will be increased which in turn leads to a life of fulfillment in your purpose here. Are we being good stewards and farmers over the seeds we have now? Or are we waiting for an increase just because.

I personally struggled and wasted a lot of time in my 20s after taking a major business loss. I didn't do my due diligence in reviewing a contract and paid dearly for it. It turned me into a person fearful with my resources. Thankfully, I stand here today transformed into a faithful servant and a great steward of all that has been given to me. I'm not sure why many of us become so focused on living a mistake free life. I've met others who have inspiring stories that consist of running full steam ahead to whatever they fear. While the results may vary, it's a strategy free from regret. A strategy that focuses on learning fearlessly instead of operating in fear. Dr. Seuss was rejected by 27 publishers before he got his first publishing deal. Walt Disney was rejected by 301 banks to finance his dream. Free yourself from regret to arrive empty.

A famous quote from the 1800s novelist and poet George

Eliot states, "It's never too late to be what you might have been." So many people don't figure out their purpose before they leave this Earth. It's simply not the design for you to arrive to heaven with things inside of you that you never birthed while on Earth. You were born to give the world something special and give glory to God. It's our responsibility to do everything possible to make sure we complete the assignment of God's will.

This chapter felt somewhat dark after I read it back; but, I felt it was necessary to provide closure for this book. It can sometimes be uncomfortable to discuss death, life insurance policies, and wills. When you discover your purpose, you are not afraid to die because you can recognize your contribution. Just the thought of me making my final transition without completing the things God put on my heart is an unfathomable thought. Imagine God revealing to you during judgment all of the great things He planned for your life, but you were unable to get over that toxic relationship, drug addiction, or childhood trauma. That would be one of my greatest fears, sitting in front of God as He tells me what could have been in my life had I pursued His will consistently or prioritized my relationship with Him.

There will be so many activities I give my time to that have nothing to do with my purpose. I have to remind myself that God's work is a priority. I am pulled in so many different directions in my career that after a day's work, I don't even want to talk. But I have something flourishing inside of me that excites me to complete. Something that I must finish to see what God wants to do next in my life.

In a recent interview, DJ Jazzy Jeff stated, "Die empty, don't die with anything creative left inside." He was referring to many musicians in the music industry who hoard music. Instead of releasing songs they have recorded that they may not be the most confident in, they only release music they receive instant great feedback from. It has been rumored that Prince had over 1,000 unreleased songs when he passed.

DJ Jazzy Jeff believes that unreleased music can inspire others. After Tupac Shakur was murdered, over six albums were released in his name over the next 10 years. Anyone close to Tupac stated he had an insane work ethic. Many believe he recorded so many songs because he accepted he wasn't going to live a long time because of his lifestyle. Commit to releasing anything you have created with the proper rollout.

Outside of Work

Arriving empty is not solely measured on work and career goals. There are so many grandparents who pour life lessons into their grandchildren that change their family lineage for generations. While you can do well after finding your purpose in the kingdom, what about your purpose in your family?

In my family, we operate at our best when everyone does the role they are best fit to complete. Arriving empty can mean setting up a family structure based on biblical principles, then, teaching your kids and family members how to operate within it successfully. If you were to journal the activities of a household that produced four college graduates, you can then teach other families how to accomplish this task.

Studies show that most people in the final stages of terminal illnesses have common regrets of not spending enough time with loved ones, working too much, and focusing too much time on the future. Use what you have learned in life and pay it forward. We are in the age of information where you can record or document so much of what we learn and pay it forward. Empty that Louis Vuitton suitcase of information you have acquired over a lifetime and pour into an individual in need.

Living with purpose has profound, long-lasting effects on your life and the lives of those around you. While the initial focus of discovering purpose is often personal fulfillment and aligning your daily life with your values, over time, the impact extends far beyond the self. It influences your personal growth, shapes your relationships, and allows you to contribute meaningfully to the wider community. Understanding these long-term impacts can provide a deeper appreciation for why the journey of purpose is worth pursuing and why it's important to communicate it.

Why Communicate Your Purpose

Your purpose should not remain hidden. It can help motivate and enliven others when expressed outward into the world. By communicating it openly to the community, it provides opportunities to meet like-minded people, assist those in need, and make tangible change. There are a myriad of ways you can express it authentically whether through work, relationships, or creative projects. But the great thing about it is no one can do it quite like you. Your approach can be impactful in a way that only you can prepare for it. The kingdom is counting on you to bring your unique abilities to the forefront and change the world. Sharing your purpose doesn't need to mean making grand public statements. It could simply involve living your purpose each day, offering unique insights to people you come across, and creating space for others to find their own sense of meaning.

Finding Your Voice

To effectively convey your purpose, it's crucial that you find your own unique way of expressing it – this could include writing, speaking, mentoring, volunteering or simply being present for others. Consider what mediums best suit your communication style. Pour into someone else who you may feel led to share with. Everyone is not a Ted Talk speaker or great with mentoring teens at the local high school. Your voice may be becoming an author or creating a YouTube channel. Discovering your voice should be a reflection of the last time you felt most at ease sharing your ideas. Was it through writing, speaking out loud, or other forms of expression? Think about how your style could help share your purpose with others. For instance, if writing is what speaks to you, starting a blog or journal about your journey might do just the trick. Set yourself a small goal over the next month of sharing it this way. Find comfort in the easiest form and continue to do this for your lifetime no matter your age.

Building Purposeful Connections

Living life with purpose often brings out people with similar values and passions. Establishing a community around your purpose can provide invaluable support and guidance; creating it gives an opportunity to learn from others, collaborate on meaningful projects and foster an everlasting sense of belonging.

Consider joining groups or attending events where people with similar interests can meet each other. Seek mentors to guide your journey, and become open to mentoring others who are in search of meaning in life. Going through this life journey with someone who has the same goal of arriving to the heavens empty can encourage you and help hold yourself accountable.

Remind yourself with the phrase "arrive empty" to live a life that is not solely focused on oneself. To truly find meaning and purpose in life, one must prioritize their relationships with others and the impact they have on the world around them. Say at work you have a set amount of tasks to complete and you complete them, then you leave feeling accomplished and fulfilled. Arriving home gives a similar feeling as completing the things that you set out to do for during the day.

Aging creates a sense of urgency to fulfill our purpose and legacy. If we lived forever, why do anything? Most people would be lazy thinking there's always time. People reach their career pinnacles in their 40s because they feel the biological time clock ticking. Similar to some women who sense the urgency to get married and have kids only because that's not something they can do after a certain age. These are goals to check off their life checklist.

Check off your purpose and operate at your optimal level. Get out of the circus and live in your purpose! I hope to one day be able to operate so greatly in my purpose that when you see it, you are inspired. Thank you for reading.

KEEP IN TOUCH!

@bwillpraise

@bwillpraise

www.ingramcontent.com/pod-product-compliance
Lightning Source LLC
Chambersburg PA
CBHW061808120626
46550CB00005B/2191